A LONG WATCH

COMMODORE AJITH BOYAGODA
as told to SUNILA GALAPPATTI

A Long Watch

War, Captivity and Return in Sri Lanka

HURST & COMPANY, LONDON

First published in the United Kingdom in 2016 by
C. Hurst & Co. (Publishers) Ltd.,
41 Great Russell Street, London, WC1B 3PL
© Ajith Boyagoda and Sunila Galappatti, 2016
All rights reserved.
Printed in the United Kingdom by Bell and Bain Ltd, Glasgow

The right of Ajith Boyagoda and Sunila Galappatti to be identified
as the authors of this publication is asserted by them in accordance
with the Copyright, Designs and Patents Act, 1988.

A Cataloguing-in-Publication data record for this book
is available from the British Library.

ISBN: 9781849046404

This book is printed using paper from registered sustainable
and managed sources.

www.hurstpublishers.com

For the crew of the Sagarawardene on 19 September 1994, and for all the lives lived—and sometimes lost—in the course of a long war

—A.B. & S.G.

This book was written in daily memory of Tom Schofield. It is also dedicated to him

– S.G.

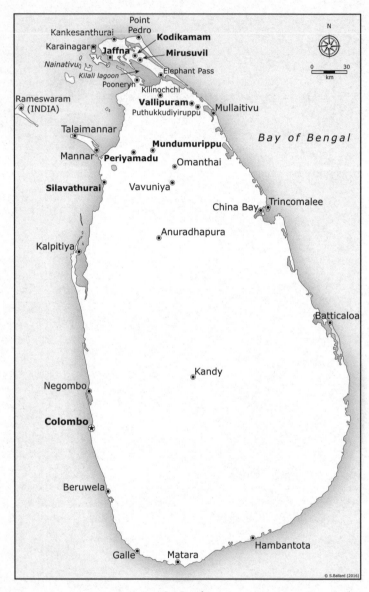

Sri Lanka

PROLOGUE

Nowadays I introduce myself as a retired naval officer. I don't say more than that. People search my face, puzzled. 'Haven't we met before?' I mention my name and they feel sure we have. 'It's such a familiar name; I know your face; where did we meet?' If they won't drop it, I say, 'maybe you've seen me on TV' and let a bit of the story tumble out. But I've only ever given a vague account. 'How did they treat you?' I'm asked. 'They treated me well', I've always said. We move on to other things.

When I came back I tried, in a way, to say as little as possible. I wanted to be the man who had left eight years earlier. I didn't want my wife and children to feel any more alienated from me than they did already, after such a long absence. I wanted to seem familiar around the house. I was not, of course. To this day my boys will go to their mother before they come to me about anything. I am the father who did not see them grow up.

When I first came home, it took a month or two before I could even move without awkwardness. I had grown used to having a sentry standing by. If I wanted to go to the toilet, back in my own home, I would look for someone whose permission to ask.

Out in the world, some people had decided I was a hero, others had me down as an infamous traitor. In a day I had been flown from my jungle cell to a tea party with the Prime Minister.

PROLOGUE

For so long forgotten, suddenly I was surrounded. But I had been through the opposite transition eight years before when I, a ranking naval officer, realised I must quickly learn the humility required of a prisoner. I used the memory of that first transformation to undertake the one I now faced, a prisoner who had to think of himself again as a man in the world. In this too, I risked coming apart.

Occasionally my wife would hear me answer someone else's question and say 'I didn't even know that'. When people asked questions they usually did not want long answers. They didn't want the answers I gave them. If I had said I was put in an underground cell, I was put in a dog cage, I didn't have a square meal in eight years, I was lashed, my fingernails were removed to extract information but I still didn't divulge anything? Then I think they would have been interested. It could have worked out well for me. But even if I had been treated that way, I would never have said it.

I made a decision when I was released from captivity that I wasn't going to help make things worse. Over my career I had seen divisions between the Sinhala and Tamil communities deepen enough. I wanted no further part in creating a cause for war. So when people asked me how the Tigers had treated me, I always said they treated me well. This was also the truth—my experience only fluctuated according to the goodness of each individual guard.

This is how I feel about it. Of course it was not a situation I would have chosen. Of course it was an experience that hurt me in ways I cannot heal. But I was a prisoner of war and the treatment I received was as good as I could have expected in the circumstances.

I could see when I came home that people did not want to hear the story I told. I had been a prisoner of one of the most ruthless terrorist organisations in the world yet I couldn't tell a ruthless story. People talk about the LTTE all the time; I lived with them for eight years and no one—not even my own naval command—ever wanted to hear my account of what they were like.

I know mine is not the only story. I have heard screams coming from underground cells. But this is my story, such as it is.

PART I

1

When I joined the Navy, I had bathed in the sea but never been in a boat. A school sportsman who had neglected his studies had few choices for a white collar job. I could become a planter, a sub-inspector of police or an officer cadet in one of the forces. This is how it was in the 1970s.

I liked the naval uniform. As a young boy, I had seen sailors in their square rig and duck cap lining the streets as a guard of honour for a *mahanayake's*[1] funeral. The impression had stayed with me. The Navy seemed the most ceremonious of the forces. Living in the hill country, I had seen them least. There were plenty of policemen in Kandy town, where I grew up. And there had been Army trawling the countryside after the southern insurrection in 1971. In everyday life, both had a bad name. I was set on joining the Navy.

After I finished my A-level exams, a friend showed me the notice. It called for applicants wanting to become officer cadets in the Navy. He thought it would be a good job for me. I agreed and applied straight away. There had been boys from my school who had gone into the Navy before, but I didn't make any enquiries. I just focused on getting in. I didn't stop to think about what the life would be like. I didn't even bother to look up the salary; I knew I would be better paid than other public servants. It was the glamour that drew me.

This was 1974, three years after the military had been surprised by an insurrection in the South and just before rebellion began to gain ground in the North. A separatist movement was about to emerge in the name of the country's Tamil people, out of growing resentment against their domination by the Sinhala majority. There would follow a long war between the Sri Lankan Government forces and these Liberation Tigers of Tamil Eelam. I had no idea. When I applied to join the Navy, I was twenty years old and had no thought or intention of dying for my country.

I didn't tell my parents I was applying. I wasn't concealing it from them; it just wasn't something we discussed. You see, in those days it was different. My parents only ever came to my school if they had been called in, or if we'd asked them to come to a cricket match. They didn't follow us around. It was up to us to wash and iron our own clothes.

My older brother had recently started working for Ceylon Tobacco in Kandy and now my time had come for finding employment. I chose between the professions I knew about. When I was called for interview I told my parents about it. They were happy with my choice—this was a respected profession—though I would be the first to leave home for long periods. My father accompanied me to my interviews. My naval colleagues still tease me about the fact he was seen holding my hand to cross Chatham Street.

I remember those journeys to Colombo. When we got as far as Kadawatha, the air would get heavier, hot and salty with the sea. You would see crows sitting on the wires of the tram lines. In those days the crows in Colombo were different from the crows in Kandy. The Kandy crow had a full black crown, and moved more slowly. The Colombo crow was an ashen, wiry, city crow. I don't know when there stopped being two types of crow.

* * *

On 10 September 1974, I came down to Colombo from Kandy on the morning train, to join the Navy. In general, we only ever went to the capital to fulfill a specific purpose and then came straight back. Recently, I had been coming to Naval Headquarters for interviews. We were the fourth intake of officer cadets and the Navy was a small enough force that even the Commander knew us all by name. Most of the other cadets were from schools in Colombo. Then there was myself from Kandy and two others, from Kegalle and Kalutara. We were twelve in total. At the time we thought it a superb coincidence that we were all Sinhala Buddhists.[2] We had that majority feeling.

That first day, we arrived at Naval Headquarters on Flagstaff Street to sign our enlistment papers. We handed over our birth certificates and gave the names and addresses of our next of kin. They drew up a personal file for each of us.

We were taken to a base nearby, at Kochchikade, where we would spend the day before we left on the night mail to Trincomalee. To kill time, a junior officer was assigned to take us out on a boat, to give us our first taste of the life ahead. It was a chance for an officer to show off his sea legs to a group of new recruits. He took us just out of the harbour so we could feel the sea beneath us.

Whenever I'd come to Colombo for cricket matches we'd made a point of going to see the sea. But this was the first time I'd actually felt its rolling. None of us threw up on this first trip, though we would make up for it in the months to come. I felt no trepidation: I was excited. Back at the mess, a sub-lieutenant spoke to us about what we would find in the Navy; what it was all about. I don't remember what he said. I don't think we understood, anyway. When they told us to enjoy our stay in the dockyard, we didn't detect any sarcasm.

We were all still civilians, some with immaculate hairstyles. In the evening we were taken to Fort Railway Station. We piled into one compartment and the train pulled out of Colombo towards Trincomalee on the north east coast, where the Navy's other main base was located. I remember when we passed the Maradana flats one of the boys waved out of the window, hoping his girlfriend—now his wife—would see him.

We had met at interviews but we didn't know each other. Some of the Colombo boys knew each other at least by sight. The three of us from outside the capital had to do our best to break into the group. On the train, we all stayed up, excited. It didn't feel like a whole night.

2

We got off the train in Trincomalee, thinking we were officers. A voice said 'Cadets, come. Line up'. We were lined up with our baggage and taken to an old bus. It was a regular bus, with the door at the back, now assigned the duty of transferring naval personnel to and from the dockyard. It was not what we had expected.

We were taken to the Gun Room—the cadets' mess, far away from the officers' mess. We got to see our dorm. I had a lower bunk in a corner of the room. The bunk above me went to the man who later became my best friend. Throughout our training we would share cabins. My friend would turn out to be the best cadet of us all—destined for the top from the very start.

Two of us, in ties and all, were dispatched to collect our breakfast from the general galley—the sailors' kitchen. As we tucked into a paang baagey, pol sambol and beef curry[3]—an ordinary breakfast—our high expectations began to falter.

We were each given a set of uniforms. The Number 1, as it's known, is a ceremonial dress, with sword. What we got was the Number 2, which is the same uniform minus the sword. There was the Number 3, which is a mess-jacket with cummerbund and black trousers. The naval uniform I'd never seen before, the Number 4—the Action Working Dress—was the uniform in which we'd spend the most time. It is a pair of dark blue trousers with a lighter blue shirt, its long sleeves rolled up.

Then, there was the Number 5, all in white: long trousers and a short sleeved shirt. There was a variation on the Number 5— the 5a is the same white shirt with shorts and stockings instead. This last was later scrapped by the Navy—some said because it exposed the sailors' scrawny legs. But I liked that uniform. It gave you a feeling.

Each set of uniforms was dumped into a white kit bag. We had to haul these around the dockyard on our shoulders as we continued our tour, still sleepless from the night before. These breaking-in rituals are practised in forces all over the world.

On the second day some people were still combing their hair. We were taken to visit the famous barber Jothi. Jothi was a legend in the Navy, one of the oldest workers in the dockyard, who considered himself an admiral on account of his years of service. After Jothi's haircut, one of our number collected his hair together and had a last look at it.

* * *

Every morning we were woken at five. We didn't have time to wash, just to get the night out of our mouths. We were taken with other training officers for a run along the road, before we gathered in the parade square for morning physical training. All of this was inside the naval base, an area large enough to have its own slopes and give us a workout. Afterwards, we had until seven-thirty to finish our ablutions and have breakfast. Then we heard the piping that meant we had to be back at the parade square for morning colours. These—a routine of marching, squad-drills and pack-drills—started at eight o'clock sharp.

We had to move on the double, each one responsible for everyone else. If one of us was late, all twelve would be punished.

But most of us had been cadets and sportsmen at school and didn't struggle with the stream of physical demands. We preferred the rare days when we were given bread for breakfast instead of string-hoppers[4] because it was slower to digest and would keep us going longer.

We had classes in seamanship, navigation, engineering, maths and damage control, before a 45 minute lunch break and more classes. At four o'clock we met in the grounds for sports hour— our favourite part of the day. After a session in the gym we'd get to play football or hockey, our batch coming together as a team to play other trainees. Or we'd get to go for a swim in the sea, off the dockyard's Pepperpot Pier.

We had to get back to the mess to change and eat by seven-thirty and then prepare for the night round by the duty officer, at eight. They would always find something you'd done wrong. Perhaps you'd forgotten to polish the undersole of a boot at the arch of the foot where it can still be polished. We were lucky if we weren't handed a punishment to carry out the same night. When the lights went out at ten-thirty, most of us passed out immediately.

At night, some of the boys wrote letters to their girlfriends under their bedcovers. I had a girlfriend who lived in the same housing scheme back in Kandy, but I wasn't one of the writers. I wasn't homesick. I didn't look out for parcels of goodies from home.

We would sleep soundly for as long as we could. Sometimes at night the seniors would break into our dorm and create a deliberate mess, pulling off bedclothes and scuffing the boots we'd just polished. We would then spend the rest of the night getting the place ship-shape again. This was another breaking-in ritual that everyone accepted. But the seniors would leave behind a bottle of arrack[5] for us to enjoy when the hard work was done. We were allowed to smoke if we carried our ashtrays with us but cadets were not supposed to drink. It was a rule we had fun flouting. On board ships, when we were used as waiters at naval parties, we would siphon whisky from the trays into bottles we saved for later.

* * *

You ask me exactly how our lives changed. I think the emphasis on punctual routine was the main difference. For everything, a time is given. You work to the time. Your system gets used to it. In civilian life you don't always brush your teeth the same way. In the military, you must. There's a reason they recruit so young. Very young people are quick to adapt; they can be moulded. I saw older direct recruits struggle because, unlike us, they knew what they were missing. It didn't take us that long. If anything, I would say that the transition out of the military, back to civilian life, is a little harder than the transition into it.

But at that point in our lives, we were simply going to grow up in the Navy. All we really missed were friends and the company of girls. Later, when we got to know each other, we could at least replace our friends outside with each other. And life changed quickly, which kept us on our feet.

I never thought about the lifetime ahead. One phase simply replaced the next. I was proud to be in the Navy. I never felt that I couldn't bear it and had to quit. But when I was about to be forced to miss my first leave to serve a punishment, I took matters into my own hands with a schoolboy trick.

Three of us had our first leave cancelled, for sharing answers on an exam. I had been away from home for six months—the longest period yet. I was determined not to miss out. I got one of my batchmates, as soon as he was home himself, to send a telegram to the Naval Academy with news that my father was ill and my presence required. When I learnt this would have to be verified by the local police station in my hometown, I got another telegram sent, to say my father was worse. I was promptly granted leave.

One day, while on leave, I went out for the day and returned home to hear that a policeman had visited. He'd asked for my father and my sister had naturally answered that our parents were both at work. The policeman, realising what had taken place, went away, saying these things were common in the service academies. He said my father and I were to report to the police station the next day. My secret was out—I had of course never told my family about the punishment or the cancelled leave. My father was not pleased. He told me this was not how we did things. But he also took a few days leave from work to back up my story and didn't make me return to Trincomalee till my holiday was over.

3

For the first six months, we were trained on shore. Then we began to train at sea. We lived on board—moving from vessel to vessel—but in the Sri Lankan Navy you're always close to shore. We served on ships that had seen more of the world and of history than we had. I remember our biggest frigate at the time, the SLNS *Gajabahu*, which had fought in World War II.

The cadets' mess on board was in the Gun Room, which is on the foremost part of the lower deck. It's the hardest place to keep seasickness at bay because that is where you feel the sea's rolling the most. Everyone gets seasick, but some much worse than others. I was alright after a few months, distracted from my seasickness by the tasks I had to perform. But there are seamen whose stomachs turn when their ship is alongside a pier, not even sailing. They spend their whole careers suffering. Some had to be brought ashore on stretchers and given saline. I remember a senior officer who couldn't sleep in his cabin. He would bring up his pillow and a traveller's quilt and lie down on the bridge. He couldn't even raise his head. He issued instructions lying down.

When we talk about getting your sea legs it isn't simply about adjusting to the rolling and pitch of a ship, although that is difficult enough. To acquire your sea legs is also to get used to a very restrictive life on board a ship. There is limited space and very little fresh water. In my time—before our ships had filtration plants on board—if you ran through your supply of water, you just had to wait till you got back to land.

* * *

There's a quartermaster on board a ship who mans the gangway. The quartermaster can be identified by the pipe around his neck. This silver pipe, which hangs by a silver chain, is named the boatswain's call. The quartermaster performs hourly piping routines and rings the bells. There is a practice on ships of ringing bells every hour or half hour. On board, routines are always signalled by bells. On land, sometimes by shouting. That was the main difference. Apart from this, drills on land were kept as on board, in case—in the shift rotations from shore to ship—a sailor should forget where he was.

These are traditions that have come down centuries of naval history. You want habits so ingrained you perform them even on land. It isn't to punish young cadets that cleanliness is made paramount, for example. It's that you can't have disease on board a ship. It's very important that the ship's bilges don't fill up. What collects in the bilges should go from there to the keel and be discharged. Fire and flooding are traditionally the greatest risks to a vessel. To check the ship is safe from these hazards, a thorough round is made at 8pm, to secure it for the night. Every hour after that, the duty watch has to perform checks. A cigarette tossed carelessly on the deck could cause complete destruction.

I see sense in tradition. Strong societies have traditions to keep them strong. There are reasons for things. Sailors salute with their palm inward because there is little water on board and their hands are often dirty. For hundreds of years the splicing of the main brace has been rewarded with a tot of rum. I enjoyed these things.

And our naval practices are just that: a set of long-held traditions. If you strip tradition out of a navy you're left with nothing.

* * *

Our life as cadets was not glamorous. One of our first journeys abroad was to Madras. We spent the whole of the long day's journey chipping rust from the steel deck of the ship and painting it, working in the hot sun all the way there. Once in Madras we were given the opportunity to go out and explore the city when we were not posted on watch. We had come on shore carrying cloves and bars of *Lux* soap to sell. We had heard they were in high demand in India and could fetch a good price on the black market. We carried our cargo off the ship and set off to meet a Sri Lankan friend who was studying at Madras University and lived in the suburbs. But the smell coming from our bags was strong. Local policemen boarded the train behind us, following the scent. We had to get off at the next station and make a run for it, escaping into a city we didn't know. Eventually, after selling our cargo to the first bidder, we found our way back to the dockyard.

We went further afield too, posted on merchant ships for additional training. We took tea to the Middle East and brought back lentils. We took rubber to China and brought back rice. In Egypt we came into Alexandria in the north and to Port Said on the Red Sea. When we remained in port for any length of time we would get every other day off. Ports are built for sailors and so there are always bars around. Once, we made our way across the desert in jeeps to see the Pyramids. We wanted to ride camels and then go to Cairo. We all agreed we could not leave Egypt without seeing belly dancers. We learnt where to go, with the help of a taxi driver. Cairo was already a big city in the mid 70s, but not very developed. It had a Cleopatra feel.

In Libya, I remember life-size cut-outs of the young Gaddafi. He was very popular then, in Tripoli and Benghazi. Two of us nearly got ourselves arrested in Tripoli. On Sundays there was no unloading so the second officer and I fancied getting off the ship to go for a morning's jog. We began our exercise with no idea where we were going. We only wanted to run on land and shake off our sea legs. But someone was following us on a bicycle. At one point he stopped us and asked questions in Arabic. We gave random answers in English. His body language was hostile. I said to my colleague, 'let's turn around and walk back'. The man followed us, clearly telling us we should come with him instead. When we were within 100 meters of the ship I said 'run!' In Sinhala, we called out to the quartermaster to lower the gangway for us and then raise it again as soon as we were on board. Once safe, our bravado returned. We shouted and gestured mockingly at the man on shore. Later, we discovered that on holidays movement was restricted in the harbour. We'd strayed into a forbidden area.

This was during the Cold War and many spies were believed to be moving through the Middle East. Suspicion ran high. Another officer went into town on his day off and began asking people to photograph him in front of things. He was promptly picked up with his camera and taken for questioning by a plain clothes policeman. Almost no one spoke English—you'd have to be lucky enough to find an officer speaking English or it would be the lock-up.

We didn't really know anything about the places we visited— we could be breaking the law without knowing it at all. There were lots of restrictions on movement—these didn't feel like free countries. But for us these trips were about exploration and discovery. We were helped by some universals. Harbours are generally laid out the same way. Similar cultures spring up around harbours, wherever you go. The difference is only in the level of sophistication in each place.

I remember on my first Suez crossing, the rest of the crew teased the newcomers—myself and the Chief Officer's wife—that the banks would be so close you could reach out and pick apples. Merchant ships were more relaxed than naval ones. They offered us some fun and a change of pace. We also got extra pay from the shipping corporation, paid in dollars. I spent the money while I was away and never saved anything.

You see, the Sri Lankan Navy isn't a blue-water navy. We used to joke that we joined the Navy not to see the world but to see Trincomalee and Colombo. It only takes a day to make the journey between the two, and you remain in sight of land. It was on merchant ships that we learnt to navigate by the stars. For this you need a steady platform and a ship that is out at sea. A month's voyage on a merchant ship would give us training, a break and a little extra money. Perks like these fell away after war broke out.

I was a boy when I joined the Navy. I had left home for the Navy and it was through the Navy that I learnt how to be in the world. The very first year of training is the one that changes your life. The rest is tough enough—leave is occasional and short—but I was never bored by life at sea. Time stretches at sea so your best hope is to find it interesting.

4

In the early days, the Navy mostly performed the duties of a coastguard. We ran short patrols in the waters around Sri Lanka. We were looking for smugglers and for fishermen in trouble. Things were friendly. There was a lot of bartering in good will. Fishermen would pass fish to our boats in return for precious water or a hot meal. You see, there is no value attached to a fish at sea, it only becomes valuable when it reaches land. Similarly a bottle of tap water is treasured at sea.

These gestures were spontaneous acts of goodwill. I remember fishermen holding up fish and waving us over. They felt the Navy was protecting them. Human contact is precious at sea. We would get closer to lonely fishing boats just to check they were ok. It wasn't only here, either. I remember when I was on a training course in the UK we once patrolled herring boats in the North Sea. There were restrictions there on over-fishing and no small fish were to be caught. The Royal Navy would board trawlers to check their catch. When they did, they'd carry a bottle of wine or whisky with them and probably come away with a return in herring. These were never forceful transactions.

Of course, later this changed. In Sri Lanka, it changed as our culture became more mercenary but it also changed with the war. It became a game of intimidation. When you are fighting between communities then everything becomes a part of asserting your power. The Forces would assert their power over fishermen and the LTTE wanted the fishermen to be hostile towards the Forces. There was also suspicion and risk now associated with getting close to unknown vessels. It's difficult to explain how sad it is that we underwent this change. It is painful to see how we live now, because I remember what it was like before. It could take generations to reverse it. But I have some faith. I've seen moments of reversal even at the height of war.

Smuggling was rife. Velvettithurai on our northern coast was called a smuggler's haven. Japanese-made electronic goods not available in India were smuggled across from Sri Lanka and saris brought back. People from the south of the island would go to Jaffna to shop for saris. Sometimes there was a trade in spices; sometimes a trade in gold. Boats carrying gold would leave from Beruwela or Negombo on the west coast, and make their way north.

This is how it works: a country's territorial waters generally extend 25 nautical miles from its shores. It can have exclusive rights to the economic resources up to 200 nautical miles from land. Where the borders of countries are closer together or further apart, particular agreements are drawn up. In the case of India and Sri Lanka a midway point marks the boundary.

You could generally find smuggled goods by searching the fishing holds of a vessel. Gold was easier to hide and much harder to find. But empty boats were always suspicious, as were boats departing at odd times of night. Fishing boats would gather in particular locations—where the shoals of fish were that night. Our suspicions were raised when we saw lone vessels set apart from the rest. Once you studied patterns, you could also predict the timing somewhat. So, we would set off around those times and operate our radar.

The routine was to challenge a suspected boat. Generally, they would stop. Or they would rev a high speed motor. Then you knew something was wrong anyway, since there was a restriction on the horsepower of outboard motors. A naval party would eventually board and search the vessel. Sometimes we'd find fish and tackle piled on top of smuggled goods. We'd then have to seize the boat with its crew and bring them ashore, to hand them over to the customs authorities. Gold smugglers you would only really catch on information. Rival groups would tip us off.

In general, gold smuggling—the highest value transaction— was done on trust. Once the goods were received, the money was remitted to the sender. The courier was of paramount importance and was paid a fixed fee for his service. If he absconded with the gold he would be blacklisted and lose his livelihood. However, sometimes gold that did not arrive was found to have been declared to customs. Then the traders would know it had been intercepted and the courier was not to blame. Sure enough, there were instances in which officers would join with the smugglers. They'd fail to declare a find, in return for a profit.

I was once contacted, through a friend, by some people looking for gold that had been intercepted but not declared to customs. All they wanted was to get the gold back so that the transaction could be completed. They told me when the gold had been intercepted and gave me the number of the naval craft that had done it. The trader was willing to buy his own gold back to keep his business credible. They were willing to cut me in on the deal, giving me half the value of the gold.

I told them they had contacted the wrong person. But I was at the time acting for the Command Operations Officer who was on leave, so I was able to access the records. I saw a boat that had gone out on the day in question, without sailing orders. The voyage was listed as a trial run, for which sailing orders are not required. But the boat had gone out very early in the morning, an unusual time for a spontaneous trial run. No one working naval routines got up extra early by choice. The boat had gone out with a very small crew and been away some time.

I asked a friend what he thought I should do. Should I confront the junior officer in whose name the run was listed? My friend said if I felt the evidence was strong I should instead file a proper report. I reported the case to the Area Authority. The Area Authority took it to the Commander of the Navy, who in turn contacted the state Criminal Investigations Department.

At the time, the Navy took cases like these seriously. I don't believe enough evidence could be found for a court martial but the suspected officer was immediately transferred from Colombo to Trincomalee, as was I. He was not promoted. Sometime later I noticed a comment in a guest book where, with considerable sarcasm, he thanked me for my help in holding back his career.

There were all kinds of smuggling and intimidation on the seas. Sri Lankan fishermen used driftnets to trap their catch. Bottom trawling fishing vessels from India would encroach into Sri Lankan waters, cutting right through those nets and scooping up as much of the catch as they could. They disrupted people's livelihoods as well as the ecosystem. It was not unlike what is happening now. We couldn't have stopped them without apprehending them in their hundreds. All we could do was to make token arrests and hope that would have some effect.

These are the things we did before the war started in earnest. After that, it was weapons we were looking for. The smuggling went on but the goods changed. I never intercepted any arms smugglers myself, but it did happen in those days. After some time, the goods changed again. Boats were now ferrying people out of Sri Lanka: whole families packed into small, perilous vessels, looking for any safe haven.

SHORELINE

5

I was away when I read the news—'Colombo Ablaze!'[6] In July 1983, I had just got married and gone straight to my next training programme, in Southampton. Being out of the country I didn't focus so much on what was happening at home. But I got that '77 feeling.

In August 1977, I had been at home on embarkation leave when race riots broke out. Tamil people were being attacked and killed by Sinhala mobs. I was at the home of one of my mother's colleagues from the teacher training college where she worked. My mother's friend was a Sinhala woman married to a Tamil man. They had lived in their village for years. Even so, we had to persuade their neighbours to leave them in peace.

The same night at about nine o'clock, back at home, we heard the mobs coming and thought of our own Tamil neighbours. They were a mother and two daughters—the father and son were working in Zimbabwe at the time. With the confident self-importance of a young naval officer, I got up. I told my father we had to go and help them. We ran to their house, arriving just as the mob did. Shouting in Sinhala, we managed to dispatch the mob. But even after they had left, we couldn't get the women to trust us and open the door. We broke down the door to find they'd locked themselves into in an inner room. They were holding on to each other and to their pet dog, all trembling.

My father, my elder brother and I led them from their house to the house next door. Both houses were at the same elevation so we could creep through the fence between them, unseen from the road. The neighbours readily took the family in. But a few days later we took them to a Hindu kovil,[7] for everyone's safety. We later heard that they had been taken to Jaffna from there. We had all lived in the same housing scheme for years but we had not really known them.

When I returned from England in August 1983, people were fleeing again. My leave was cancelled and I was posted north. I travelled on a ferry carrying people from the South to the refugee camps the Government had set up in the North. They were people from Colombo who had first sought shelter from the riots at the Ramakrishna mission in Wellawatte and at the kovil in Bambalapitiya.[8] From there, they were transferred directly to the North. These were people going with a sense of resignation. They did not want to arrive homeless but they wanted to leave. Some may have had family in the North but others did not. Many of these people had probably lived for generations in Colombo.

Still, going to live amongst a majority of Tamil people may have seemed a safer prospect than the homes they were leaving in a majority Sinhala south. The ship was crowded. People with connections got access to the crew's facilities. Others made do with temporary toilets on deck. They were all travelling to be offloaded at Point Pedro at the northernmost tip of the island. They knew little more than that about their future. Later people were to do the same again—maybe even some of the same people—fleeing the North, across the sea to Tamil Nadu. Each time, they were just trying to get away from the present trouble they were in.

Never after this could I take issue with the idea of a Tamil homeland in the North.[9] If Tamil people were not safe in the

South and were safe in the North, then that was their homeland—the Government had conceded that. I remember taking
trains from the South to Jaffna when it was still possible to do
that. The carriages were quiet until we reached Vavuniya. It was
north from this point that people would start talking. It felt to
me that only then were they comfortable; from there on they felt
they were in their own country amongst their own people.

There had long been a Task Force for Illicit Immigration to
guard against people from South India entering Sri Lanka ille-
gally. Eventually, movement began to go completely the other
way. It was not emigration really, it was exodus. People were
fleeing Sri Lanka in terrible conditions. On naval patrols we
would find whole families and their goods packed into small
precarious vessels. We saw that it must have been worth risking
everything just to get away. As servicemen we knew what was
happening on the island. We knew if we brought them back,
they'd have to be sent to a refugee camp where they would suffer.
Sometimes an inner feeling would say why not let them loose
and let them find safe haven somewhere. Then we would turn a
blind eye to these multiday fishing trawlers—packed with 20–30
people—converted to the business of human smuggling.

6

My first posting after the 1983 riots was to the tiny island of Nainativu off the northern Jaffna peninsula. I was to be in charge of the naval detachment there. It was here I also made the arrangements for my wedding later in the year.

I had met Chandani the previous December, in Colombo. The annual Navy Day Dance—an officer's ball—had come round and I needed someone to go with. In an all-male force we were always short of women friends. So the boys with girlfriends would ask them to bring other friends to events. Chandani was one of these friends.

It so happened that in the months after we met, I was posted on a vessel that was being modified in the Colombo dockyard. Because I was not going away again, Chandani and I had a chance to get to know each other. On 1 June 1983, we had our marriage registered. I was due to leave for England for training the next week. The wedding itself was to come in September. As it turned out I could only get brief leave to attend my wedding and return to duty in the North.

On Nainativu, I was meant to safeguard the Buddhist Nagadeepa temple and its priests. Buddhist pilgrims from the South had actually stopped coming to Nagadeepa a few years before. Reports of robberies and killings in the North had filtered south and people were frightened to make the journey. But the priests never vacated the temple. They were the only Sinhala people on the island but they had good relations with the local community, who brought them their alms. The head priest was a very strong character. Even the Tigers left him alone.

So, in fact the priests were in no danger, but here was a risk the Government felt it could not take. If the temple was attacked it would stoke fires in the South. The truth is that through nearly thirty years of conflict the government prioritised what the southern people wanted. These were the sorts of things to which they paid attention.

The priests didn't want our protection as such, but we were sent to provide it. After we got there, the Navy took over provision of the priests' alms, which they had previously received from the community around them. So, in a sense we broke that relationship a little.

In addition to the Buddhist temple on Nainativu there was a big Hindu temple, patronised by people from the mainland. The island itself was almost bare, with patches of scrub and paddyfield; occasional palmyrah trees standing tall against the horizon.

The people who lived on the island were a quiet community of educated public servants, who worked on the mainland, as well as farmers and fishermen. The farming community could only cultivate their land according to the rains, growing sesame in one season and rice in the other. It was a hard living they made and they concentrated on surviving.

The islands were still relatively untouched at the beginning of the war. There was no real strategic advantage to the LTTE in taking over Nainativu, so we moved freely there. Our relations with the islanders were cordial. They were cautious, of course— afraid of being punished by both sides. These were people who struggled between a real sympathy with the LTTE cause and a need to survive under the dominant power, which was at that time the state.

The situation for Tamil officers remaining in the Forces was especially peculiar. I knew one officer who couldn't visit his parents in Jaffna. There was a simultaneous fear of forced conscription by the LTTE and of raising the eyebrows of southern intelligence. The fear of being suspected by your own command was the biggest problem that Tamil officers had. Many opted to retire around this time.

You can't entirely blame the authorities either—they carried the memory of the southern insurrection in 1971, when some support for that movement had been discovered inside the Forces. So there was a natural suspicion, coupled with the reputed stealth of the LTTE operation. Officers did sometimes sell information as well as military hardware—but these could as easily have been Sinhala officers.

* * *

In the very late 70s we had already stopped going out into the town. We started moving in convoy—even to go on leave. Then petrol was banned in the North—to prevent it being used to make bombs—and only diesel was allowed in. Fuel convoys were run from Anuradhapura in the north central province—to supply the military at its bases. But the thirteen soldiers being ambushed and killed in 1983, even before the escalation that followed—was enough to bring everything to a halt. After this, when on land, we were simply confined to barracks.

Gone now were the days when fishermen from Mannar would sail to South India to go to the cinema and come back after the show was finished, slipping through the docks undetected. There was such a thing as an Indo-Lanka Railway service then, with a regular passenger ferry between Thalaimannar on Sri Lanka's Mannar island and Dhanushkodi on India's Rameshwaram island. We used to like being on the pier when it came in, just to see people come and go. We'd loiter there and chat with the ferry master. This was in the early days. Later, it was required that a naval vessel should be on patrol to monitor arrivals and departures. From then on, we were not there to chat but to carry out surveillance checks on the passengers. We were looking for illicit Tiger movements and transfers of goods. After 1983, the ferry just stopped operating altogether and our lives also changed drastically.

There was no ground movement for us in the North anymore. naval movement was by sea and there was Air Force movement in the skies. It was exactly what the LTTE wanted—to separate us from the people of the North, so that they could take charge.

We servicemen had enjoyed travelling to Jaffna before. We had friends in the town—friendships passed down generations of servicemen, since the naval base was established in the 60s. When we were posted north, we would look forward to parties at people's homes and to eating Jaffna cooking. We worked a tropical routine when we were in Jaffna, which meant we clocked off at one o'clock in the afternoon and could have a few drinks before lunch. For young officers, this was a big deal. We'd go to our friends' houses and fill up on Point Pedro vade.[10] Our friends would come to mess parties. We all moved freely between military and civilian worlds.

We'd eat idli and thosai[11] at the Subash Hotel and go to see a film, returning on the last bus of the evening. We watched whatever was playing, even traditional Bharatanatyam dance. Going out was really a way to break out of an all-male camp and see girls.

In our vehicles we'd make a point of patrolling the streets at the time schools closed for the day. Sometimes we'd adjust the nozzles of our windscreen wipers to turn outwards and spray schoolgirls with soapy water as they passed on their bikes. It was meant in fun but we didn't really think it through.

At that time, uniformed people were accepted. Gradually of course this changed. It changed with the LTTE's politicisation of the Forces and it changed with the things the Forces did. People started trying to avoid the military. There came a point when our friends outside didn't want to talk to us and we were also reluctant to contact them. As young officers we were sad about losing our fun.

7

My story as an adult goes hand in hand with the history of the war, as it must.

I was twenty years old when I joined the Navy in 1974; a Navy the public only saw on Independence Day and special occasions. In the same years that I had been growing up and preparing for adult life, the Tamil nationalist movement had been grouping and re-grouping. As the story goes, in 1975, Alfred Duraiappah, the Mayor of Jaffna, was shot dead by a young militant. I was then caught up in my early naval training. In 1976, the Liberation Tigers of Tamil Eelam, or LTTE, was formally con-stituted as an organisation, under the leadership of that very same young militant. His name was Velupillai Prabhakaran and he was a year younger than I was.

There had already been big changes in the 70s and there were more to come. I'd grown up in independent Ceylon. In 1972, that turned into the Democratic Socialist Republic of Sri Lanka. My parents were strong supporters of the incumbent socialist Govern-ment, led by the Sri Lanka Freedom Party, and we followed their political lead. In the elections of 1977, this Government suffered a crushing defeat. They were so badly routed they not only ceded power to the more capitalist United National Party but the place of official Opposition to the Tamil United Liberation Front. The riots of 1977 followed this election. The new Government was mistrustful of the new Opposition.

I remember being put on patrol to give security to Amirthalingam, leader of the TULF and the Opposition. Amirthalingam was in Jaffna to hold meetings about self-rule in the Tamil north. We were meant to observe the meetings and provide security. But I look back and see more in them than I did at the time. There was a story that Mrs Amirthalingam had announced she would not sleep until she had shoes made from Sinhala skin. We were still dividing and ruling, not aware how serious things were.

With an easy majority in Parliament, the new UNP Government introduced a new Constitution in 1978, moving the country from a Parliamentary to a Presidential system. The President was to have executive powers that the previous prime ministers had not, especially in declared Emergency situations. In 1979, a temporary Prevention of Terrorism Act was introduced that gave the Government further powers. Looking back now, you might say that alongside the LTTE, the Government was arming itself for war.

I was serving in Trincomalee when the Jaffna Public Library, an institution of enormous cultural significance, was burnt down in 1981. I remember we sent fire engines from Trincomalee to Jaffna, maybe over 150km away by bad road. That was our level of readiness. They were never going to save the library. The fire burned for four days, they said. I didn't go north again until I was sent to Nainativu in 1983. I served about a year there, I think. Then I was posted East again and back to Colombo in 1986.

By this point, my wife and I had our first child. My eldest son Shamal was born in April 1985. For the next four years I would be stationed on a number of vessels, but with Colombo as my base. Our second son, Manil, was born in October 1987. I was happy to be at home with my family and relieved not to be away when there was fresh unrest in their part of the country. These were of course the years of the second JVP insurrection. The Janatha Vimukthi Peramuna had tried and failed at Marxist rebellion in 1971. Now it was back in a more extreme manifestation and the Government beginning to respond in kind.

Our set-up at home was that my wife and the children lived with her parents in Colombo, since I had often to be away. I would come and go. These were bad times. I remember one day we drove past Bellanvilla temple with the children. There had been killings the night before and there was a corpse still burning in a tyre. The children, very small at the time, saw it too. Shamal later told his grandmother he'd seen a cyclist who'd had an accident.

The Army had moved south to confront the JVP and the Indian Peace Keeping Force took their place in the North. Sri Lanka had been pressured by India to accept their help with our escalating conflict. I remember being in Trincomalee and seeing the Indian forces arriving. Troops came in shiploads and on daily flights to China Bay in the east and Kankesanthurai in the north. We were not happy about being put into barracks and ceding control to a foreign power. We had to get their permission to go anywhere. But with the IPKF naval officers themselves we had cordial relations. We knew many of them already. We had trained alongside them when we'd been sent to India for training. Inside barracks they were ok with us, if not so much outside.

In the South, a crackdown began. Police DIG[12] Udugampola, notorious for a brutal approach to rooting out the JVP, shifted his attentions to Kandy in 1988–1989. I was worried about my younger brother who was then a student at Peradeniya University. The flowered hillside campus, just outside Kandy, was a hotbed of JVP unrest. I found my brother temporary employment at Citibank in Colombo so that we could have him closer at hand. Anyway, the university was closed on account of the troubles.

The JVP had a very strong presence in Colombo harbour. When they asked the dockyard workers to stop working, they stopped working. If an urgent need arose, it was up to the Navy to step into the breach. This was how I came to get a call from Dr Gladys Jayewardene in September 1989. Dr Jayewardene was Chairperson of the State Pharmaceuticals Corporation. A container consignment of medicines had come into port. The dock workers were on strike and would not unload it. Moreover, the shipment was from India and the JVP, opposed to the Indo-Lanka Peace Accord, was asking the public to boycott Indian goods. But the hospitals were short of medicines and Dr Jayewardene wanted this consignment distributed. She contacted the Commander of the Navy. He contacted the Western Area Commander. It was he who in turn called me—I was told that this job needed to be done and that it needed to be completed overnight. The consignment had to be unloaded and removed from the port to a warehouse. I was told to speak to Dr Jayewardene directly to get the exact details. I spoke to her and assured her 'Madam, we will see that the job is done'.

But that wasn't going to be so easy. I still needed harbour employees to do the unloading. They were willing to work but afraid of the consequences they'd suffer from the JVP for doing so. I struck a deal with them that they would pretend to be working at gunpoint. I then got together a crew from the Navy. We went into the harbour and seized some container movers. Under Emergency regulations, the Services could do things like this. There is a lot of scope for malpractice with Emergency Law but occasionally you get the chance to do some good. We took the container movers in convoy to the area where the ship was berthed. We had the consignment unloaded and then drove it straight out of the harbour. By morning the goods were in the warehouse.

I called the Area Commander that day to tell him the job had been done. This must have been conveyed to Dr Jayewardene because she then called me to thank me for it. All this happened in the morning. I was thrilled to have taken on the challenge and to have succeeded. But the glow lasted less than half a day because when Dr Gladys Jayewardene went home for lunch that day, she was shot dead. It was either on her way to lunch or her way back to work from it. I saw it on the news.

A day later I received a note in the post, addressed to me and copied to the Commander, thanking the Navy for a job well done. Gladys Jayewardene had signed it—I always wonder if it was the last thing she did before she died. I felt very, very sad. One by one we were losing our intellectuals, our better administrators and our more straightforward politicians—the people who might have done this country some good. Vijaya Kumaranatunga had recently been killed, now Gladys Jayewardene.

To me, she sacrificed her life not to do herself any good but to do good for others; those without the means she had. I'm sure many others would not have taken the risk. I'm sure many people advised her not to, warned her there would be repercussions. I remember it as a period of terror. It hung in the air. People couldn't take the coffins of their dead for burial. People could not switch the lights on in their homes.

You ask if we felt fear in the services. We didn't know how to, yet, I think. Northern terrorism was still in its infancy. The fear of attack was only just beginning to seep into the military. The JVP's 1971 insurrection had been swiftly dispatched so we had not fully registered how different it was, this time.

Sure, it did cross my mind that after paying Gladys Jayewardene back they might also come for me. I had had threats before, since I'd broken strikes in the harbour and sometimes even publicly addressed dock workers. At that time, I carried a pistol even in civvies. So the sense of threat was there. But we still thought we were at home in the South, whereas we felt more vulnerable and alien in the North.

It's also this: 'danger' does not really exist as a concept in the military. A man going into battle must do so unaware if he is to do so at all. So, he is put into continuous training until he operates without thought. You give a soldier a gun and tell him he can do anything with it. Somehow it does not register that he could take a bullet just like the one he is firing.

Terrible things happened. In 1988–89 there were constant patrols bringing people in for questioning. I remember two guys who had been beaten so badly the instruction was to kill them and get rid of them. I intervened with the junior officers who had been put on the job—I told them killing is easy now but it will be bitter afterwards. I said take your orders but don't kill them. Let them go and tell them never to come back this way.

I think at that time the Forces handled the LTTE and the JVP in very much the same way—they did some killings, then came back and said 'job done, everything under control'.

After all this, we saw the Indian Peace Keeping Force depart, three years after we'd seen them arrive. Both the LTTE and the Army moved into the space they vacated. I was posted back east to Trincomalee. I must have been there when the LTTE evicted the Muslims living in the North in 1990, but I don't remember it as such, I have to say. That was a few months after the LTTE killed 147 men and boys attending prayers in a mosque in the eastern town of Kattankudy.

In 1991, Rajiv Gandhi was assassinated. We knew it had to be the LTTE that had done it. Only the LTTE was capable of that sort of mission at the time. I can't say I shed many tears. I never felt that Rajiv Gandhi had been a friend to Sri Lanka. He had led India in encouraging the separation between communities in Sri Lanka. Here he was, reaping what he'd sowed.

I was stationed back in the North at the time—in Karainagar, which I will tell you about later. My youngest son Lahiru was also born while I was there—in 1992. I had been in Colombo for Shamal's birth and Manil's birth, but this time I could not get away. My wife actually drove herself to the hospital when she knew she was going into labour. She had herself admitted and then called her brother to ask if he could take the car home.

When President Premadasa was killed in 1993, I was stationed in Tangalle. Most people wanted him to go—so this also did not come as much of a surprise. Even within the Navy, there was some relief. As a sailor or officer you have to follow instructions but inside you still think and feel as a citizen. Your personal ideology doesn't change, even if you have always to serve the ruling party.

I remember an incident that happened at the beginning of this posting to Tangalle, the year before. Our recent President, Mahinda Rajapaksa, was at that time MP for Hambantota. He was leading a *pada yatra*[13] south from Colombo, in protest against forced disappearances by the UNP Government. The water supply to the Rajapaksa home in Beliatta was suddenly disconnected by the municipality. Mrs Rajapaksa came to see me. She was running a nursery school and there was no water there. She made a request for a bowser of water to be sent to the house. I agreed to do this, without requesting permission from anyone else. If I had been asked about it I would have described it as a humanitarian office— sending water to children. But of course I knew I was also sup- porting the *pada yatra*—in line with my personal support for the then Opposition. It was not impossible, even within the forces, to make small decisions according to your own conscience.

8

One moment stands out for me as the most formative of my military career. This was in Karainagar, on another of the northern islands, immediately after our military operation there in 1991. Dealing with the civilian sick and weak you really feel the effects of war.

In April of that year, I was awaiting transfer to Jaffna, eight years after my last posting to the North. I was summoned a month early because the naval base at Karainagar was under siege. The news in the east, where I was when I received the order, was that the camp was about to be overrun by the Tigers. Apart from the sea route, all other approaches were under siege. The news we received by radio reported heavy mortar attacks on the base at night. When I left Trincomalee, many of my colleagues did not even want to shake hands with me and wish me good luck. They felt I was going to a certain death.

We left at night, journeying in a gun boat along the eastern coast and around the top of the island. We sailed from Trincomalee past Mullaitivu to Point Pedro and on to Karainagar by morning. Sea access was secure and the Navy patrolled the Karainagar channel. As we approached the base, I saw casualties being removed and taken to the nearby Air Force base at Palaly.

Other personnel were going off shift—we were on a regular relief vessel going to remove troops and deploy new ones. The men leaving told us there had been a lot of bombing the night before and we should expect more that night. I was to be second in command at the base.

There is a routine even in these things. During the day there was generally a reprieve from fighting. There was better cover for the LTTE at night, when they couldn't be seen from the air, so this generally was when they attacked.

They were attacking with locally made mortars, the Baba-mortars known as Pasillan 5000 and Pasillan 2000. The numbers indicate the count of iron pellets inside the mortars. These are like the balls in a ball razor and are dispersed as shrapnel when the mortar explodes. This was custom made LTTE ammunition—cased in aluminium that had usually been removed from the floorboards of buses. But these mortars had to land directly on their nose to explode. Often we recovered unexploded mortars in the morning. In fact, most were wasted. Later on, they improved their technology.

For several weeks, as I remember, the bombardment went on almost every night. Towards the end of April, we broke out of our defensive position. At dawn, air force bombers bombed the perimeter of the base to clear the way. Then armoured vehicles broke through the LTTE defences. Infantry troops followed. As Army troops cleared the ground, Naval troops took up position. We lost a few men and a few others were injured. There was a strategic importance to not losing this base. It was also what the Navy did—simply to hang on.

After the operation was completed we emerged from our base. We realised then that the LTTE attack had not itself been that bad. I'm not sure it was much more than a few guys lobbing mortars at the base. But we saw a different kind of destruction when we came out.

In Karainagar, everything had been broken open. It felt like ninety percent of the houses had been forced open by the marching troops. It was here I really saw the mentality of a Sinhala army walking through a Tamil village. Whatever they saw, they destroyed. Wardrobes had been opened, clothes pulled out, family photographs smashed. The cattle and the goats had been let loose. I saw cows inside houses. You know, I think anyone returning to one of those homes would not have thought twice. If they were young, they would enlist with the LTTE.

People had been directed to move to the temples. The Army announced the instruction. Any marching army, seeing a figure moving inside a house, will fire at it, out of suspicion. But the code is never to open fire on a religious shrine. So that is where people were told to congregate. It was also for easy scrutiny, afterwards.

Within a few days, the Army had control of the island. They would also take charge of screening civilians, to root out any LTTE infiltration. But I could see other kinds of aggression. So, when they asked for the segregation of men and women I objected, fearful of what could be in store for the women.

I told my superior, the Northern Commander, that the Navy should intervene. The ultimate responsibility would be ours so we should intervene now. Although the Army was in charge of the military operation, the Navy would be responsible for the security and welfare of the people. I said the actions of our colleagues would be our burden to bear, so we should take charge from the start. I suggested that families should be kept together at all cost. I think people only feel secure with their families, not even with their neighbours. It was established that the naval commander in charge should make the final decisions regarding civilians.

Gradually the soldiers began to vacate the island. We had a big issue with troops removing loot as they left. I told the officers in charge that they must take control of their troops. The talk at the time was of '*yudde* + *sudde*', warring and clearing.

The looting was systematic. The troops knew that the shrine rooms of houses generally contained the family safe. So, this was what they broke into, looking for gold. I had heard about looting of course. But this was the first time I saw it with my own eyes.

Just imagine: your house is intact today. Suddenly you're told to vacate it; go to some place. After a week or so, when you return, you find a ransacked house. How would you feel inside? A life's earnings maybe, gone at once. Maybe the work of generations, undone.

Take a family album: it doesn't mean anything to a stranger. A little book. But to you it is a treasure. There can be a lot of memories kept safe inside. Now all those memories have been desecrated. Maybe the memories of generations. Gone with just one album.

I remember some casual talk after dinner when I asked a few young officers why there was so much looting. Why did they let their troops do this? I asked. Weren't they clearing the way for Prabhakaran? They told me a long story about how soldiers needed insurance in case they lost limbs to anti-personnel mines. I told them—'look here, you don't have to worry about your soldiers' limbs. There is a government, there is a ministry. They are responsible people who will look after the welfare of your soldiers. You don't have to rob civilian people'. Even to tell such a story was to set a bad example to their men and to each other.

They argue that at war these things happen. Maybe. Maybe. But if we are trained and honest soldiers we should at least correct the troops we each command. If some of us managed to do it, it wasn't that it couldn't be done—but that people didn't want to. Was it that they benefited too? Or was it just the easier option?

It was standard Navy practice for troops to be checked for stolen goods before leaving a place. Sure, troops complained about being mistrusted. But it was just another drill, like checking a gun. After any firing practice you have to demonstrate that both the gun and your pockets are empty. It's a safeguard, nothing to get hurt about. Gradually these procedures were commuted, on the grounds we were in a war situation. But wrong is wrong, whether you're in peacetime or at war.

I couldn't stop the looting but I could stop the troops taking their stolen goods off the island. The soldiers were to be transported in naval vessels so I issued an instruction that nothing other than their military belongings should be allowed on board. Heaps of goods had to be dumped on the pier. They collected in great piles there. There were wedding photos in frames amongst the goods left on the pier. These were photographs of strangers, taken from the houses of strangers, as far as the soldiers were concerned. So, it was not just about money. I don't know how you start to explain these things. There were children's toys, bicycles, just about anything. Initially it seems to be a rational theft and then it becomes something completely different— collecting trophies of war. Perhaps when you are ordered to destroy things, you develop an instinct to spoil everything.

9

When I left the island a year later, the loot was still there lying in our stores. There was no way of finding whose everything was. Occasionally someone would come and claim something that could be identified. Or they would replace a missing bicycle with one that had been abandoned. But a great many things remained. I think perhaps a lot of it belonged to people who had left. Within a couple of weeks of the military operation most of the people who lived on the island had deserted the place. Others did not to want to look too hard for things they might not find. Things had changed. You can't assume the things that matter to you in peace-time will be the same ones that matter in a time of war. Was I embarrassed to bring people back to the stores, you ask? Of course I was embarrassed. It is embarrassing to bring people to a place and ask them to identify their own looted belongings.

People were still living in the temples. Then, after about two months, they returned to their lives and started repairing their houses. We resettled people slowly because the houses were in real need of attention. At first, we let people leave during the day and see to their houses, returning to the shelter at night. It was also a way to reduce the impact of the destruction, letting people get used to it bit by bit. I was second in the chain of command.

But because my superior was also the northern Area Commander, I was left in charge of the day to day administration of Karainagar.

After the battle, only the old and feeble really remained in Karainagar. About three quarters of the population had left the island—for the mainland or beyond. In fact it was in this connection that I first encountered the ICRC;[14] the International Committee of the Red Cross. One day, a Red Cross delegate came to the island, with enquiries from people on the mainland. They had asked the ICRC to find out about family members who were still in Karainagar. We summoned people to the temples again to exchange information with the ICRC. I liked that the ICRC came. It gave us an opportunity to prove our credentials. We could show that things had been done right; there hadn't been extrajudicial killings or other abuses.

At the time I felt that the re-unification of families was a must. Of course later I was to feel it for myself—that the living should know whether their kin are alive or not. To me, the category of being missing in action is the worst state to which we can lose a human being. Nobody can really go missing—they are either dead or alive somewhere. In a natural disaster it is possible to lose a dead body, but not in a war.

There was anti-Red Cross propaganda then too, of course. What made it worse was that people in the South had seen the value of the ICRC during the JVP insurrections, so it was a bit rich to oppose their work in the North. It was a 'murderous army' in the South and a 'heroic army' in the North, doing exactly the same thing.

Yes, it did get passed around that Boyagoda was soft on people and that this would be good for the LTTE. They thought I should have been a more suspicious administrator, rooting out terrorism in the civilian population.

But I thought it was our duty to strengthen people materially and morally, and try to win back a peace. I felt I needed to prove to them that I was not their oppressor. If I did it, then the others would too. The services are designed to remove people's initiative and make them followers. One man makes the decisions and the others follow, that is what gives the whole thing structure.

This was on my mind when I carried vegetables and medicines back to Karainagar from my turns of leave in Colombo. But mostly I just felt it was the need of the hour. It was less important to carry things for myself—I would be well fed at the camp anyway. But in the town of Karainagar not even a Panadol[15] could be found. Later on we conducted medical camps and opened a dispensary. I am proud of the work we did there.

This was the only time I had managed an administration on that scale. Karainagar is on the biggest of the islands off the Jaffna peninsula, elevated from its island status by the building of a causeway to the mainland. Named after its trees, it was more fertile and more populated than the other islands. Yet the people who now remained were the more elderly. We worked a tropical routine which meant I was off duty by lunchtime and could leave our base, alongside the pier.

I would go for an evening stroll and call on people. It became such a routine that some households would miss me if I didn't come. Sometimes I think I was an echo of a son who had left the island. That gave me satisfaction, in a way. I remember the apothecary Dr Ambalavanar and his wife, who would prepare plain tea and vade for me every day. If I missed a day the doctor would say 'Amma[16] was waiting for you yesterday'. Much later, I heard that this gentleman may have been killed, in unexplained circumstances.

I'm still in touch with one of the children I knew on Karainagar, now in her early 30s. She was a small kid who came up and talked to me at the ICRC meeting in the temple. I was struck that she was not shy or fearful, talking to a uniformed officer.

Hers was also a family I visited in the evenings. Apparently I gave her one of the bicycles that was lying in the yard. Years later, after my release, I was at Naval Headquarters and I saw a girl and her father sitting in a waiting room. Something rang in my mind. She also seemed to recognise me and I saw her asking one of the sailors something. Afterwards she came up and said 'you're so and so, no?' In the decade since I'd seen her she had passed her A-levels and was now looking for employment. I was able to help her find some, which also meant something to me.

Many people who left the island just abandoned their houses in their desecrated state. Many of them have never returned to date. I know some families in Colombo and in Vavuniya. They're not yet ready to trust this peace. When you're really broken and broken-hearted, it takes a lot to start again.

But there are people who do. When I was posted on Karainagar, after each leave to Colombo I used to carry medicine back for a gentleman there. He lives in Wellawatte now. His children are resettling in Canada and the UK. His youngest daughter is just migrating and his wife has also left the country. But he says he wants to return to Karainagar and settle down in his own home.

SEA

10

Late in 1993, I joined the SLNS *Sagarawardene*. The *Sagarawardene* was, at the time, one of the Navy's two largest warships. The *Jayasagara* and the *Sagarawardene* had been named to incorporate two halves of a previous President's name. In name, each ship was dedicated in part to the President and in part to the ocean itself.

They were 40-metre Offshore Patrol Vessels, newly built in the Colombo dockyard. They operated from Trincomalee in the east. With trawler hulls, travelling at a speed of 15 knots, they could remain at sea for longer than the next class of Chinese vessel we had in the Navy, which had been gifted to Ceylon during the 1971 insurrection.

In general, at this time the Sri Lankan Navy would have to berth a mother ship in the ocean which could refuel smaller ships. These smaller vessels would return to it periodically for refuelling. The mother ship, a converted cargo ship, also carried high-definition radar surveillance equipment and could direct the smaller, quicker vessels. It would point them to areas of suspicion. But time was naturally lost in the trips back and forth. And the mother ship, stationary and visible, was obviously vulnerable to attack.

You have to remember we were no superpower. We didn't have a lot of high definition technology, just small boats with low profile systems, patrolling a vast area, with limited visibility at sea. There were constant technical and weather problems and it was a matter of doing our best with makeshift arrangements. The need for refuelling was, of course, what had made our island itself an important stop on east-west shipping routes.

The *Sagarawardene* was not a high speed vessel, but one with good stability and reasonable accommodation. It did not need to feed off a mother ship. There were just three decks on board; the messes below the main deck and the flying bridge above. Both the ship's bridge—or control room—and my cabin were on the main deck. A crew was assigned to a ship for six months or a year. I captained the *Sagarawardene* for a year, with the same crew of 45. As one always must, on board a ship, we worked closely together. We officers worked a four hour shift, followed by eight hours off. I had worked with most of the sailing crew before, at one time or another.

Our main mission was one of patrolling and surveillance, monitoring LTTE transmissions. A few things happened in that year. The Tigers launched a major attack on the Army and Navy camps near Pooneryn, from an unexpected approach over the Jaffna lagoon. Over two hundred soldiers were killed in battle and a similar number went missing. The LTTE themselves lost around four hundred cadres. Some of the Government soldiers caught in the battle, I had transferred from Kayts to Pooneryn about a month before. I thought of them as soon as I heard the news. I was at sea at the time and sought permission to get closer to the battle, but my commander did not approve it. We were in shallow waters and there was a fear the ship could run aground. Originally built for commercial patrol, it had less manoeuvrability than a purpose built warship.

The first half of the year we patrolled the east coast and then, responding to monsoonal changes, we shifted to the west. I had recently completed twenty years in the Navy. This meant that for the first time in my career, I had the option to apply for retirement. I had already decided, a year or two before, that I would take this option. I had been in the Navy a long time. I thought it was time to come home. I had a middling sort of career, without specialisation, and I wasn't expecting major promotion. The Navy was also becoming less like the place I had joined. I could leave the force and find a job in the private sector, I thought. By now, the private sector was a regular option.

I applied for retirement. My application was rejected by the Commander. Officers could not be spared. I was told to try again the following year. I could have requested to have my commission withdrawn. But that would have required the approval of the President and meant I couldn't carry my rank in civilian life. It wasn't an option I considered. Things looked good for me. I would probably succeed then next time; I only had to wait another year. Anyway, I was due to be posted home to Colombo for that year, after my final voyage on the *Sagarawardene*.

11

We set off on the morning of 18 September 1994 from Colombo harbour, escorting water-jet boats to our base at Kalpitiya. We were there by midday and, that night, ran an evening patrol along the north western coast. We anchored off K-point. It was around eight o'clock that evening, I think, when the monitoring people told me they'd detected some LTTE movement. They'd intercepted some transmissions about a planned attack and heard the sound of boats moving in water. I decided to weigh anchor and move hurriedly away from the shore.

The next morning we came back to Kalpitiya to meet the boats we were supposed to escort onwards to Mannar. On this run I noticed the RPM dropping and the exhaust temperature rising, which suggested we had an exhaust leak in the trunkings of one engine. We shut off that engine and just ran on the other. My Engineer suggested we should attend to this problem as soon as possible. Ours was to be a ten day patrol and we were down to a single engine on day two. So, after dropping the boats off, south of Mannar, we anchored at the One Kaala Reef, as we called it, or the 1¼ Fathom Reef. This was still the morning of the 19th and our next assignment was to escort a fuel convoy north from Kalpitiya on the morning of the 20th.

We had to wait a while for the engines to cool down so we could begin work on them. A routine repair, easily done by the ship's watchkeepers, still took the better part of a day. We planned to set off at six o'clock that evening. We would work our way down the coast on patrol, making landfall in Kalpitiya early the next morning. But when we were discussing it in the Ward Room, my Executive Officer suggested to me that perhaps it would be better to stay where we were and do some further monitoring of LTTE transmissions. We could set off around midnight: it was about a six hour run and we would still arrive on time. I thought this sounded like a good idea, given the previous night's warning in Kalpitiya and the upcoming fuel convoy. It would please our monitoring team. They always complained that it was impossible for them to work unless we stayed close to land—it was only at close range that they could intercept clear transmissions. I thought this new plan seemed like a better one.

My Executive Officer was on the eight to midnight watch, and then I would take over the next watch. I told him to wake me up before he started the engines. There was a bright moon that night and it lit the sea immediately around us. As I walked away, I looked out at the water and saw there were a lot of fishing boats around us. I came back and told the Ex-O to keep a good look out. On a moonlit night we would be like a beacon on the water and the LTTE could use the fishing boats for cover and get nearer to us.

I said goodnight to him again on the bridge and made my way to my cabin. I just lay down in my clothes, as is naval practice, and picked up a *Newsweek* magazine I had there. I read a few pages and fell asleep.

I woke up again because I had been thrown out of bed by something. The clock in my cabin showed the time as 11.20pm. I rushed up to the bridge, thinking we had run aground on the reef.

My Executive Officer met me as I reached the bridge:

'Sir, *apata gahuwa*,' he said, 'they hit us'.

* * *

I said 'who?'

He said, 'LTTE'.

Coming up on to the bridge on the starboard side-wing I looked back. I saw the whole stern of the ship had been ripped off. There was no stern at all. The ship was taking in huge quantities of water and appeared to be sinking.

I hurriedly sent teams downward to see if we could control the damage at all. They couldn't get very far—soon they reached a gaping hole. The ship was sinking, stern down, with the anchor keeping it in place.

So, it was riding on the anchor and tilting down. The men could only try to rescue any survivors from below. You see the attack had taken place just below the mess where most of the sailors were fast asleep at this time.

The explosion had also knocked out our generator power. I sent the Electrical Artificer, Perera, down to the battery room to try and disconnect the batteries and bring them up to the bridge.

We had four main armaments on board. One gun was ripped off; the other forward gun—a 25 millimetre gun—couldn't be operated without power. So I only had two manually operated 5-zero—50 calibre—guns on the two wings.

But tonight, the gunners were so agitated they forgot that the gun barrel needed cooling time. With a belt-fed weapon, if you keep the trigger pressed, the whole magazine will discharge in a few seconds, really heating up the barrel. And with an overheated barrel, the rounds get jammed in the chamber. When I saw this had happened with one gun, I had to tell the gunners to stop and fire the other gun in a more methodical way. With this one remaining gun we managed to fire at one of the oncoming LTTE boats. It exploded before it reached us. But there was another boat. Our rounds were ricocheting off this second boat, which suggested it had armour plating. Just as we connected the batteries to the radio to try and raise the shore, the boat rammed us, causing the next explosion.

* * *

With the second explosion the ship caught fire. It started sinking rapidly.

We couldn't even access the small arms in the armoury, because the armoury was under water. And really everyone was in a state of shock and confusion. I think if we had seen the enemy boats approaching and begun a battle with them at that time, it could have been a different story altogether. But here, while the captain and sailors were asleep, a sudden explosion had surprised us all. The surviving sailors who emerged from the mess came out on deck in a state of shock. The enemy had won three-quarters of the battle already.

Yes, it really was chaos. One sailor started distractedly throwing our life jackets and rafts into the sea. It was as though he was thinking too far ahead. There was no one in the sea to catch these floats, we were all still on board at that time. Our battle must have lasted thirty to forty-five minutes and it was only towards the end of it people started regaining their wits. This was when the second explosion struck.

The ship began to look like it would go down completely. What were we doing, fighting for a sinking ship? The water had come up to the level of the bridge when I made the decision we should abandon ship.

By this point it was as though we were all in one room. The bridge area was the only place clear of the water: the bridge and the flying bridge. From here we could simply step into the ocean. I was, I believed, the last to leave the bridge. At this moment we were just escaping a fire.

12

We were already at sea level. We had only to jump from the ship and grab on to a raft. There were about six or seven of us holding on to the last raft and I the last to join them. I told the other guys we must paddle away quickly in case the ship were to go down—as at the time I thought it might—and create the vacuum that sinking ships sometimes do. We didn't want to get sucked into that.

We were now in a dark sea and an oil spill, the water thick with diesel from the exploded ship. On the surface of the sea your vision is not that good—you can't see things at a distance unless you are at an elevation. On the surface of the sea, you become very small. At night you can really only see the objects immediately around you, in this case debris from our ship. Through the fireworks of gunshots, we could make out the shapes of LTTE boats moving around. We could trace the silhouette of our own ship, listing on its anchor.

We were soaked in diesel ourselves. We were moving away from the ship but we didn't know in what direction—whether towards the shore or further out to sea. We spent about half an hour drifting with our float, watching an LTTE boat in the distance. One of the men—I don't remember who, now—saw that while we were all wearing our usual sea rig of shorts and a t-shirt, I was also wearing the epaulets that revealed my rank. He pointed them out and pulled them off. The LTTE were flashing their torches about. Every now and then we heard a burst of gunfire. We could only imagine they were firing at others in our crew. Or they were firing at random: just in jubilation.

Now a boat was closer, its torch skirting our float. Now coming towards us, torch trained on us. It was less than fifty metres away and a round was fired. E.A. Perera, next to me, slipped into the sea. I told everyone to scatter. The only thing to do was to disperse and each grab a hold of something floating by. You can't try swimming in a sea like that.

I don't know what made me stay clinging on to the raft. It wasn't something I thought about—maybe in my shock I didn't let go. Maybe I had some instinct it held a better chance of survival than the churning sea. It wasn't that I knew I feared death or feared drowning. I wasn't feeling anything I recognised.

Suddenly the firing stopped. They had their torch trained directly on me, the man they'd spotted holding on to the raft. They were moving towards me. I said my goodbyes. I could only guess they were coming closer to get a better aim.

But when they got closer they threw a rope onto the raft instead—a rope with a hook, which they used to drag my raft closer. Once I was alongside, two or three men hauled me aboard. I think in fact I grabbed on to their rope. I knew they were my enemy. But at the time it felt like a rescue. They fished me out of the water and laid me on the bow of the boat. With the same rope they bound my hands behind my back. I was told to stay lying down. The motorboat turned around to start speeding away.

Now I could hear the choppers coming—the Sri Lankan Air Force was on its way to the scene. I was on the bow—the platform at the front of the boat. We were moving fast on a choppy sea and I started to bounce up and down. Bound as I was, I couldn't grip the bow. I would soon have rolled off into the water. I indicated to one of the men—just in sign language—that I couldn't hold on where I was. He realised it and moved me into the boat, propping me up against the wheelhouse. I could look up enough to see the choppers.

I knew they had spotted us. On a moonlit night it would have been possible. They were hovering above us and firing. From that high up, they couldn't possibly have taken aim but they would also not have wanted to get too close to the boat, not knowing what sorts of armaments were on board. So they would swoop down in a large circle and up again. And they fired not at the boat but just ahead of the wake. That's how it is with a moving target—you can't fully make out a boat at night but you can see its white wake. You try to judge where the target is, in relation to its wake. This is what the choppers were doing. They would swoop down, firing this way. Immediately the Tigers would switch off the boat's engine, making it immobile and invisible again.

Now the choppers were just wasting ammunition and time, no longer knowing where the boat was. Eventually they would have to go up again. Then the Tigers would re-start the engine. In this way we progressed in lurches on our journey, until the choppers gave up. It was difficult to see them fly away, having lost that battle, but a relief too, not to be caught in crossfire.

It must have been about 45 minutes until we came alongside a small pier. They untied me and led me out of the boat. Two men walked up to me: one was in charge, the other was acting as his translator. They asked me—in Sinhala—whether I was wounded. I said I was not and I also introduced myself as Commander Boyagoda, the Commanding Officer of the ship they had attacked. They seemed a little taken aback by that—surprised.

Then there was a wait, but I didn't know what for. Other cadres, both men and women, came out to investigate their catch. They were full of curiosity now. One of the guys who had been on the boat spotted my gold chain. He said '*thangam thange*', 'hand over the gold'. He tugged at my wedding ring. I told him it was too tight now to take off and that it was my wedding ring. But I took off the chain, with a priest's talisman on it, and gave it to him. I gave him my watch too—which would have been of no use by then.

We waited a little longer and then I saw a jeep approach in the dark. A man got down, a hefty fellow. The interpreter said 'He's Soosai.[17]' This was such a familiar name to me and now I was meeting the man. He came and shook hands with me. I said, in English, 'I have heard you so many times over the net, I am glad to meet you'. I don't remember his reaction—at most he nodded his head. He pointed me to his jeep. I was to get in and he would drive me away.

13

I was to have eight years alone to go over my actions and the events of that night. I had repeated need of defending myself against allegations of negligence at best or treachery at worst. You know the old saying of course—the captain never abandons the ship. The captain goes down with the ship. I had made a decision to abandon my ship.

The story of the *Sagarawardene* was a story I read, long before it was a story I told. In the first few months of my captivity, I had daily access to newspapers from the South. In them, this story, and speculation about it, was drawn out over some weeks. Many rumours grew around the capture of the *Sagarawardene* and the role I had played in it. One report even went back to question the moment we were anchored to the reef, repairing our engine. It was said that I had remained in that position in order surreptitiously to supply fuel to the LTTE. I was curious why the LTTE would then have destroyed such a useful resource.

You know the story: I was found guilty of negligence by a naval Board of Enquiry while I was in captivity. My offence was to have kept my ship anchored in one place for such a long time. The verdict was passed very quickly—I think during my first month in captivity. I'm sure it was before November's Presidential election. The Navy had lost its biggest warship. There were allegations of mismanagement and carelessness being lobbed at my superiors. Someone must be to blame. I was the captain of the ship and, even better, I was not there to speak for myself. I don't think they ever expected me to return.

But to go beyond matters of protocol: twenty-two of my own crew, with whom I had worked at least the year on the *Sagarawardene*, had perished in the attack. The Navy's biggest warship was lost. I had become a prisoner. I had lost my men, my material and myself. I had reasons of my own to reconsider my actions, had it not even come to a case of needing to defend myself. The story I tell of the night of the attack is one I pieced together lying in my first cell and then in the years of thinking I've done since.

When I got my sailing orders for that voyage I met the Deputy Area Commander, as was the usual protocol, to find out if there were any special instructions for the voyage. I had been told by others that there were many fishing boats at sea at the time—despite the ban on fishing. I sought clarification as to how I should respond to this. I was told that since the Government had entered into secret talks with the LTTE, the authorities wished to build good will. The instruction was to be gentle and not to upset the balance of things. They didn't want fishermen reporting abuses to the LTTE and a consequent escalation of tensions. The LTTE, apparently, had a different plan.

The worst irony was that we had ourselves intercepted LTTE transmissions making reference to a planned attack on a vessel. The day we spent anchored at Silavathurai to listen further, the communications had dissipated. Our monitoring crew said there was less activity and we thought the threat had passed. I understand now that the LTTE had of course realised we were monitoring their transmissions, from the fact we'd escaped attack the night before at Kalpitiya. So they'd gone in for a radio silence on the subject. My first LTTE translator would later joke that we had got away with it the first night but they'd got us in the end.

What actually happened? I don't know. Later on, the divers who went to salvage the wreck suggested that the way the plates were ripped open it had to have been an explosion from underneath. That would have been the work of divers who attached underwater mines to our hull. But the LTTE always maintained to me that it was two suicide boats that made the attack—one of women Black Sea Tigers,[18] the other of men. They first celebrated successful underwater explosions some time later.

As for the battle itself, I know what you're asking. Why were we so unprepared? I was the captain of the ship. We did have standard naval procedures for battle but they were designed for conventional warfare rather than guerrilla attack. They were procedures based on seeing a convoy of ships coming your way, knowing an attack was imminent and getting set for battle. You sound action stations, people get into the action posts and so on. These things are all gone through in drills. Whereas we were disoriented when we started and already at a terrible disadvantage. In a twenty year naval career I had experienced nothing close to this.

Was I afraid at the time, you ask? I don't think I was feeling anything that I could identify. As I told you before, people who go to war don't think they're going to die. Soldiers at the front never know until they're dying that they're dying. It's not that they sacrifice their lives but that they get shot, not knowing.

I think, for myself, once we were in the sea that was itself the greatest danger. Being captured by the Tigers felt in my shock like a rescue, even at the time. I still think that: here was a sequence of events that conspired to save me from drowning.

* * *

There were mistakes I made that may or may not have changed the course of events. When I feared the ship would sink I forgot that we were in shallow waters. The furthest the ship could go down was 1¼ fathoms, not even its total height. It could still have toppled over but it would not have sunk completely, as I had feared.

I have searched my memory for anything I may have missed leading up to the attack. But my recollection always begins from the same moment: when I fell out of bed and ran to the bridge. I remember my Executive Officer saying 'they hit us'. That was the last time I saw him—I completely lost track of him after that first moment. He is still listed as Missing in Action.

But you say what about now, looking back, would I have done anything differently? I don't think so. I'm not sure if I can even think about it that way. This is how I see it, you see—we had very little chance of coming through this battle. Had there been other support perhaps we could have managed it. But we were the only ship in that place. The *Sagarawardene* would have been the only operational ship on the west coast at all at that time. The rest were all small boats.

If I had kept to my original plan and weighed anchor at six, this would not have happened. That's all I can think of that would have made it come out differently. Maybe it was our fate to be caught at the intersection of all these things.

* * *

With a crew of forty-five, leave was hard to plot and you were practically never sailing with a complete crew.

Additional Officer Ratnayake was not on that final run. His wife was suffering complications in her pregnancy and I had given him leave. We'd also left the Engineer behind to attend his own wedding and sailed with the Chief Artificer. The Senior Communicator was also on leave.

You remember the man Perera, the Electrical Artificer, who slipped off the raft next to me? He was an efficient, trustworthy character who had served with me in other places. His daughter had been very sick and had died just weeks before. Perera had returned to work just before our last voyage on the *Sagara-wardene*. The last time I saw him was slipping into the sea: his body was later recovered, with gunshot wounds.

But his case was unusual. Many men are still listed as missing in action, meaning, in this instance, that they probably drowned at sea. Many bodies did wash up on shore in subsequent weeks but, without DNA testing, they were impossible to identify by that point. The only bodies that the authorities were able to distinguish from the others were those of the female suicide cadres who had also perished.

I learnt, eventually, that two of our men had remained hidden on board and I had not been, as I always thought I was, the last man off the ship. These two men had later been rescued by naval boats—something I did not know for nearly ten years after the attack. The story I heard was that Lieutenant Devendra had hidden in my cabin and then made his way from there up to the flying bridge when he heard the Tigers coming. We'd have to ask him, to be sure.

The official list issued after the attack on the *Sagarawardene* went as follows:

18 rescued
20 MIA
2 killed in action
2 captured

PART II

14

The jeep pulled up to a house. I was led inside and seated on a bed in the dark. Someone brought me a bottle of Necto.[19] On the pier, earlier, I'd seen goods being unloaded from a boat. I could only imagine the Tigers had intercepted some food supplies from a civilian boat travelling to Mannar island. A bottle of Necto from this load had been spared for me. I was thirsty and finished the whole bottle. Then they brought me a photograph album. As they began turning the pages I saw that on each page was a different vessel of the Sri Lankan Navy. They wanted me to identify which mine had been. Ultimately, they came to the *Sagarawardene* and I said that was the one.

Soosai was also in the room and I learnt later that this was an attack he had commanded himself. They asked me questions about my ship and its deployments. They wanted to know if we had been accompanied by other vessels. It must have been about three in the morning by now. I was tired and soaked in diesel. I said I wanted to sleep. They agreed to it immediately.

My shock was beginning to wear off. As it wore off, I began to take in what I had lost. I was the captain of the *Sagarawardene*: I'd lost my men, I'd lost my ship and I had possibly lost myself.

Overwhelmed and exhausted, I slept without even trying to. Early in the morning—just a few hours later—I was shaken awake and given a cup of tea. By now my skin was burning with the diesel that was on it. Diesel mixed with sea water had made me very sticky all over. I said I wanted to have a bath. This was also granted immediately. The translator, Ananda, led me to a well where water was drawn and poured for me. I didn't have to do anything myself. I was allowed to have a good bath and I was handed a t-shirt and sarong to change into. I didn't register at the time that I was discarding my naval uniform and putting on a new uniform for the years ahead.

As we walked back from the well I saw a familiar figure crouching by a house, leaning back on the wall. Ananda asked if I knew that man. I said 'yes, that is my Leading Supply Assistant, Vijitha'. Vijitha had also been captured, he and I the only captives taken from our ship. Vijitha's story was that he and others had been floating in the sea when they saw a boat approaching. While the others had swum away from the boat, Vijitha had swum towards it. This is what I mean: it was the same human impulse that I think came over me too. We had both seen the approaching boat as coming to our rescue and the people on it not as enemies but help. Vijitha had, however, not been treated as deferentially as I was. He said *'godata genalla, dekak anna,'*—that when he was taken off the boat he was hit.

Back at the house Ananda told me we would not be here much longer; we would be leaving this morning. He did not say where to. He was friendly and I mentioned to him casually that my gold chain had been taken. I was not expecting him to react. But he told me to wait a minute and left the room. A little later he came back and opened his closed fist to me. 'Is this it?' he asked. It was. He returned the chain to me, along with the talisman that hung from it.

A year earlier, just before I took up my assignment on the *Sagarawardene*, I had received a message from a Buddhist priest.

I was stationed in Galle and while I was there I had tried to be helpful to the hospitals and temples around. The head priest of a local temple now wanted to give me a protective talisman to wear, since he knew I would be going to the northern front.

At the time I really didn't believe in these things. We used to joke that these were 'bunker *soora*'; 'bunker charms.' In an attack everyone would still run for the bunker, wearing their charms round their necks. All the same, I didn't want to refuse the priest. So I sent word back that I would come to receive the talisman. Only I did not want a big charm to wear around my neck and I also wanted one without great restrictions on what I could and could not eat. I explained that you couldn't be a fussy eater in the forces—you had to take what was given.

On the day before I was to set sail, I went to see the priest and have the ceremony performed. He said this was a special talisman—the one they call the *hena raja thailey*. There is a story in folklore about someone who carried one of these inside his arm—and became immune to all danger. The priest told me that he had tested the powers of the oil inside my talisman. I don't know that I paid too much attention but I did go through the ceremony. They incorporated my name into their chants and set me on my way. Maybe it's a coincidence that I have survived all these things since. But now I also wonder if there was something in it, after all.

But to come back to that first morning: it was like recollecting a nightmare, I suppose. Everything had happened so quickly. Now I was on shore, in this house. By morning, I realised I was a captive. I still didn't know what was in store for me. But from the way they were treating me, and from their respect for my naval rank, I somehow did not feel they were going to hurt me.

So I just waited. After a while a jeep came and I was led out. Vijitha was still there, where he had been the first time I saw him, leaning against the wall. We were both put into the back of the jeep and our hands were tied in front of us. But we were not blindfolded and we could see out as we travelled. From the movements of the sun, I calculated we were heading north.

* * *

We were given breakfast at an LTTE camp. We were taken into a house and given tea, maybe a biscuit. I didn't feel hungry in the circumstances. Then we were put back in the jeep and driven off again. Eventually we arrived at the water's edge. They told us it was the Kilali lagoon and that we would be waiting there for a while. They didn't tell us what we were waiting for. We were given lunch packets of rice and curry. I ate all of mine but Vijitha could barely eat at all. He was scared and he was worried about his wife and newborn daughter. 'Now they're going to kill us' he said. I said I doubted it but, if that was so, there was no point worrying about it until they drew their guns. Still, Vijitha fretted, as he would do for some time to come.

Eventually Soosai arrived. This time he was dressed in full camouflage uniform and looked much more impressive than he had done the night before. Today he was wearing a pistol in a holster and carrying a T56. He lifted his weapons and said 'gifts from Premadasa.[20]' With him was a cameraman who was going to film our journey for the Tigers' propaganda arm. I saw this footage years later, in captivity. By then it was like a movie; a disconnected experience of watching yourself in a film.

By boat we crossed the vast Kilali lagoon that separates the northern Jaffna peninsula from the rest of the island of Sri Lanka. It was dark by the time we arrived on the opposite shore. Another camouflaged jeep was parked there and we were put into it. Again Soosai tapped the body of the jeep and said 'gift from Premadasa'. I knew we were on the peninsula but I had not been outside a naval base there since 1983. So there was no way I could recognise the terrain in the darkness. We moved in silence. I could see the odd lamp. We may have driven a long way to go a short distance. We stopped at a house and Soosai went in. When he returned it was without the cameraman and he was dressed again in a sarong and t-shirt. I kept feeling that he reminded me of a *mudalali*[21] in a hardware shop.

We were brought to another house and told to get out of Soosai's jeep. Here another man appeared. He was a very smart guy with a crew cut and an air of authority. He must have been in his mid thirties; about the same age as Soosai. 'I am Selvaratnam,' he said, in English. He introduced Soosai again. 'He is our Commander of the Navy' he said, indicating that Soosai and I were men of the same trade. Selvaratnam—Sasikumar by his *nom de guerre*—was the head of the LTTE's reconnaissance unit and military office. He was to be my custodian for the next nine months and a powerful figure in my captivity.

Selvaratnam and his assistant Reuben now put us in another jeep and drove us on. We arrived at the house where we were going to stay. There was a room for me and a room for Vijitha. Inside, a towel, toothbrush and tube of toothpaste was laid on each makeshift bed. There were plates of food already served. They had been expecting us.

Selvaratnam showed us our rooms and then ran through a few instructions. He said we were to stay inside. He said there was no point trying to escape; it wouldn't be easy to do without being caught. He said we were not to speak to each other. But he was friendly in his instructions. He said not to worry, peace talks were coming and we would be going home very soon.

It was less than 24 hours since we had been captured. I was not as disoriented as I had been the night before but still far from normal. I wanted more rest. Vijitha was given dinner in his room and I was given dinner at the table in the hall. Then we were told to go to sleep.

15

I didn't know where I was when I woke up. I was sleeping on a board bed, without a mattress, on which a plastic woven mat and a pillow had been laid. I saw the room around me for the first time. There was no electricity on the northern peninsula—not since the war got going—and we had arrived after dark the night before. My room must have been about 10 feet by 10 feet. It had just one small window, about 4 feet off the ground. It was an old house: a small, ordinary house. I was in my room, Vijitha was in his. The main door of the house was locked but here our room doors were not locked. Outside our rooms was a passage with a dining table in it. I could walk up and down this passage. I did it for the exercise, but also to get a look into Vijitha's room and wave to him. Vijitha never came out of his room.

In the beginning, I was still a little disoriented. But afterwards, I had a sense of having arrived at a destination. The tension in me began to dissipate. I was happy to be allowed to move around the house.

In the morning, I would hear a cock crow in the trees and wake as it came down to the ground at dawn. I would tell the guard I wanted the toilet so he knew where I had gone. I would have a bath at the same time. Morning tea was brought to me and I would then wait for breakfast. A little later in the morning,

I think from my very first day, four young cadres would come to talk to me. I will tell you about them, later. At lunchtime they would leave and I would be brought lunch. The food was good in this place—the instruction must have been to treat us well. Meals would come regularly—tea followed by pittu or bread in the mornings; rice and two vegetable curries at lunchtime; iddiyappam or pittu for dinner.[22]

After lunch I would retire to bed or read a newspaper if I had one. I spent my evenings looking out of the window. I looked out on two mango trees and behind them a palmyrah fence. I could see the tiled roof of the house beyond. There were lots of squirrels and small birds outside and I would throw them pittu and watch them. That offered me a kind of mental relaxation. Every now and then I would see a cat. I could hear a dog barking further off.

I was glad sometimes to have the mild-mannered company of Mohan, one of Selvaratnam's men, who spent some time with us in the house. Mohan spoke to me in Sinhala. He addressed me as Commander and said consoling words to me. He told me Selvaratnam was a good man. Mohan seemed to enjoy recounting stories of his childhood in the South. He had started his life in Wellawatte in Colombo, and gone to school at Royal College. His family had been displaced to Jaffna after the 1983 riots. Eventually, the rest of Mohan's family had migrated to Switzerland while he had joined the movement. I imagine that it was Mohan joining the movement that had been his family's pass to leave— the LTTE sometimes extracted these bargains. But it was also something he had chosen, he said. He must have been in his mid-twenties by the time I met him. He told me that his mother despaired of his choice. She told him that he was trying to win freedom for his people by losing his own.

While Mohan came and went from the house, another cadre, Kanthan, stayed with us. He was our jailer, cook, cleaner and conversation. He asked me once if I remembered 'the fishermen' from my days in Karainagar. I realised he was referring to a particular story—where the Navy captured some men posing as fishermen and put them in the dungeon of the fort. I had seen them, blindfolded and chained together like a train. Kanthan asked me about the torture chambers at Karainagar. I said I didn't know anything about them. I didn't like the idea that torture chambers existed but I had good reason to think they might. From the way Kanthan spoke about this incident I think he may have been one of the prisoners. I didn't ask—I was cautious in those early days. Now the tables were turned, and I was Kanthan's prisoner.

The day is longer in captivity—you feel it is longer and wish for it to go fast, especially if you think that release will eventually come. The series of events that had brought us here were so sudden that I simply faced each thing in turn. I didn't search for meaning beyond that. I didn't have time to think of myself as a captive. Even looking back, the thing I find difficult to imagine is not the fact of becoming a captive but the scale of the change I had to go through. I was a ranking officer in the Navy, accustomed to the facilities and deference of the office: a Commander. Then I was a prisoner, without a name. For the next eight years I followed instructions.

In the ordinary course of things it takes a long time to change a man. But when we arrived at that first house, I had to change overnight, to survive. The state of being into which I entered could never be peaceful, but I could grow accustomed to it. I think back on that time as when I inhabited a different, and hidden, age of man.

My first morning as prisoner, I'd heard 'tttsk tttsk' at the window. It was one of the guards outside. He was trying to get my attention to see if I knew what the time was. I couldn't believe it. I was not used to anyone addressing me with a smacking of teeth. I tried to ignore the guard but he was insistent. My blood boiled. I turned to him and said 'There is a way to address an officer—I am a Commander in the Sri Lankan Navy'. The guard bridled in turn. He said 'you no commander here—you commander Ceylon Navy—here you Tamil Eelam[23] prisoner'. In his anger he had, unconsciously, cocked his rifle at me. I now thank this guard, Sridharan, for teaching me a first essential lesson. Being a prisoner was different from being a man in the world. I would have to adapt quickly.

16

It probably helped me that for the first few months there were things expected of me.

Early on, there were media interviews to give. The sinking of the *Sagarawardene* and the capture of its Commanding Officer were things for the Tigers to boast about. They distributed colour-printed flyers in commemoration. I became known as 'the Captain'.

I was put in Selvaratnam's jeep and taken to meet journalists. I remember a makeshift television studio and an interview I gave to the *Eelanatham* paper. I was asked about Sri Lankan forces harassing the public. I said I didn't allow anyone to fire at defenceless targets. They never pushed me on these matters. What I said was not the point. All they wanted to get across was that they had a senior officer of the Sri Lankan forces in their custody. Still, these were also the accounts that were translated into English and Sinhala and published in the southern newspapers. So the little information that reached my family and friends came translated through several successive agendas. Of course, I did not know at the time if they had any news of me at all. I knew they had to know about the attack on the *Sagarawardene* but I didn't know if they knew I was alive.

I was taken to the hospital within my first week. I had an earache from all the diesel that had got into my ear. I was treated by Dr Shanthini, as they called her. She was a doctor within the government health service and simultaneously an LTTE cadre. This was not unusual. Everyone who saw me at the hospital must have known I was 'the Captain', famous for being captured.

A stream of people came to see me. Dinesh came—he was the LTTE military secretary and personal assistant to the Leader. Karuna[24] came. This was in the first few days. I was too much in shock to start any conversation. I just sat there, passively. They had not come to speak to me either. They were just coming to verify the captive and get a look at him. There were also Tiger cadres who came to see us purely out of another curiosity. They had never seen these Sinhala people they were fighting. Even some of those cadres born in the 70s had never seen the enemy except in battle. I remember that government soldiers were often similarly intrigued about the Tigers.

Most days, Selvaratnam himself came to visit. He usually visited in the mornings, accompanied by Mohan and Reuben. I'm sure he sometimes spent up to an hour talking to me. I don't really think there was a purpose to it. Remember, the LTTE was actually in dialogue with the Government at this time and peace talks were due to begin. I believe that made me less significant. I think to some extent the conversations were to make me comfortable and also to keep us docile. I think Selvaratnam relished the opportunity to speak to someone on the other side. It wasn't so much that he wanted to listen. He wanted to re-articulate his own thinking and used me to sharpen his argument.

Yet he was always civil and gentlemanly about it. I never felt that he mistrusted me, even at the start. Selvaratnam didn't believe in the peace talks. To him they were just a breather, giving the LTTE time to prepare for another Eelam war. A separate state of Eelam was the goal and he would not be shaken from it. He told me that by the year 2000 the state of Eelam would be established. I felt that a federal solution would be a better one. I always accepted the causes of Selvaratnam's struggle—I had been at war long enough I could not deny them—but I insisted that I disagreed with his means. This conversation we had again and again in those early months. Neither of us changed our minds, but I believe we understood each other better in the process. We would ask each other—what is your opinion about this or that? I came to agree with Mohan that Selvaratnam was a good man, however much I disagreed with his political strategy.

I began to feel comfortable asking things of Selvaratnam, trusting he would take me at my word. I was worried about Vijitha—his spirits were low and he wouldn't come out of his room. I told Selvaratnam I needed to talk to Vijitha to keep him from sinking into depression. He readily agreed to let me bring him into the public space and talk to him there.

Over a period, Selvaratnam gradually revealed more to me. Sometimes he told me about things the LTTE was doing. He told me that the only arms they had surrendered during the ceasefire were the ones they were ready to decommission. Sometimes he gave me details of his own story. He was—like others I met—of the second generation of LTTE cadres. I believe they were a more committed group than some of the later recruits. He was from the area between Trincomalee and Welioya. His family had been displaced from the Kent and Dollar farms. His story was like that of so many others. He had experienced upheaval and displacement on account of his culture and ethnicity. That had led him straight to the movement.

17

Now, let me tell you about the four young cadres who came to see me every morning. Oppilan was the leader of the group. He must have been a teenager at the time. The other three were girls: Nala, Krishna and Mangalika. Selvaratnam brought them to meet me. He said to me 'these are our students and we want them to learn about the Navy. Tell them everything you know'. They in turn called Selvaratnam by his *nom de guerre*—Sasikumar Master. Every morning they would come to meet me and we would sit together in the hall. We sat around the table—they gave me a seat at the head and took their places around me. Oppilan would ask the questions I was to answer, with Mohan acting as translator.

They were teenagers, not experienced interrogators. They wanted to talk to me about the Sri Lankan Navy. I answered their questions. I always felt that the things they were asking me were things they could have found out very easily without me. You'd only have to look at a copy of *Jane's Fighting Ships*. There you would find the vessels of the Sri Lankan Navy listed with their capabilities, like the vessels of every other official navy in the world. They asked me about places in which I had not served for years. I would find that they were up to date with developments I did not know about.

I did not need to lie. I had never served at Headquarters, which also meant I had never been privy to any official secrets. So I answered the questions asked. I did not lie or exaggerate. A lot of the time I found that my interrogators knew more than I did. They had made a study of the Navy—I only knew how things had been when I'd last served in a place.

I did occasionally hold back. When they asked me about the naval armaments department, in which I had served in the late 80s, then I gave vague answers and elided questions. Sometimes I gave archaic information, a little deliberately. I did not refuse to answer questions. But nor was I going to be eager in giving information about my own force.

All of the questions asked were general, never operational, except that they wanted to know about the layout of the Trincomalee dockyards. They brought me a map and then they would ask me about the places on it, one by one. I imagined there were still other ways for them to get at this information. There were so many civilians working in the dockyards. They would go home at night and were easy prey to LTTE blackmail.

I remember a man who was the storekeeper of naval armaments. He was so straight he would not open the doors of the armaments to anyone—however high ranking—without the proper approvals. Yet, later I heard he had been questioned for treachery. I felt that if he had indeed done anything wrong it could only have been achieved through blackmail. I noticed that some of the books these young cadres used had in them the names of retired naval officers.

Of course, during my time in captivity there were subsequent attacks on the Navy, especially at Trincomalee. But I never felt implicated—the information the LTTE got from me was neither exact nor extensive. It would have been impossible to base an attack on that.

How it worked was this: Oppilan brought a questionnaire with him and he would work through the questions one by one. It was all done very politely—I was never threatened in any way. The girls called me 'Appa'.[25] Eventually they finished with their enquiries. Then they asked for my help in translating a standard manual of seamanship. This I was willing to do. I would read the English and explain to Mohan in Sinhala what it said. Mohan would then translate from Sinhala into Tamil. This job took some time and helped pass the days.

18

One day Selvaratnam came and told me to get ready for another journey. He put me in his jeep and drove me to another house. I was taken to a room and seated in front of an interrogator. The interrogator spoke to me in English. I was told that I was going to be tried for war crimes against the Tamil people.

I responded that the best testimony in my case would come from the people of the islands that had been under my command. From the interrogator's calm expression, I felt they had already made enquiries.

The trial was conducted by a single interrogator, apparently acting on instruction. After each question and answer I heard communications equipment operating in another room, at the back of the house. Notes would arrive from this room with questions in them. The interrogator would then pose the questions to me.

The trial focused around one set of events. They asked me about recent incidents in which the Navy had killed boatloads of civilians on Kilali lagoon. I knew about these incidents already. They had taken place while I was stationed in the South, in Galle, and I had heard about them there. It was a bad time on the peninsula. The Navy was involved in shore bombardments to clear a path for advancing troops. Sometimes these bombardments were arbitrary, made without specific targets. Then again, sometimes warnings were issued to civilians but the LTTE would not let them leave an area. But it was not the larger situation they wanted to know about—which I believe the LTTE accepted in the course of war—but specifically the attacks on civilian boats crossing Kilali lagoon.

I had not been involved. I told them I had never approved extra-judicial killings at any time in my career. They mentioned names they wanted to be revenged on. You know, terrible things did take place. Sometimes, trying to stop refugees fleeing to India, naval boats would open fire on the vessels in which they were travelling. I believe these were killings that began as misjudgements not as murders. But then sometimes, afterwards, not knowing what to do about the evidence, they would pour petrol on to the boats and burn them, with the people on them. Have I seen this, you ask? We would patrol the seas in a ring and at night sometimes you could see flames. I would ask one of my crew over the radio if something was happening and the reply would come '*nae sir, bar-becue ekak daanawa.*' 'No sir, it's a barbecue'.

But at my trial I think they already knew I had not been involved in the things they were asking me about. I was confident too. I knew what I had and had not done and by now I trusted that my captors would believe me and act on reason. Much later, Mohan told me that people from Karainagar and Analaitivu had made representations in Jaffna on my behalf. They had written to the leaders, to give testimony of good experiences dealing with me.

This trial itself only lasted an hour or two and I was served tea and sweets. Before we left, Selvaratnam came to tell me that I had been cleared of the charges in question.

* * *

Another day, when Selvaratnam came to see me, he said 'it's your second son's birthday isn't it?' I was surprised that he knew. 'Your second son is very lucky,' he said. That was all he said. The LTTE as I knew them may have been a reasonable detaining authority but they never let us forget who was in charge, especially in those early days. At this time we were also unseasoned captives and would let ourselves hope for release, on account of a statement like this.

I was told to get ready to go out. Vijitha and I were taken by jeep to another house where we were given new shirts to wear. 'We're going to a birthday party' Selvaratnam said. A little later our blindfolds were removed and we saw the board for the LTTE political office at Kokuvil. I saw an ICRC jeep parked in the compound. When we got inside they indicated there were visitors for us. We were photographed by an LTTE cameraman, with the ICRC's Head of Delegation. This picture subsequently appeared in *Eelanatham* and was then copied in the southern dailies (although it was not mentioned in the southern papers that the photograph was of an ICRC meeting).

I knew now this was not to be a release day. So, of course there was some disappointment. But there was also a significant joy in store for us. We received letters from home. It was our first indication that our families knew of our fate. There were three letters written on regular notepaper, not the ICRC forms we were all later given to use: one from my wife and one each from the two of my sons who were old enough to write. My wife had written very little, nervous of this new system. She only asked how I was and reassured me that she and the boys were ok. My elder boys, at seven and nine, were still struggling to understand what had happened. They asked if my ship was still broken and how soon would I be able to come home?

After we'd read our letters, the ICRC registered us and gave us ICRC numbers. They enquired after our health. They wanted to know if we had been injured. They asked what our living conditions were like. We said everything was ok. They said they would try to meet us once a month.

I missed my family and I was really so happy to get letters from home. I was also relieved to have been registered with the ICRC. I tried to reassure Vijitha that this at least was some safeguard for our lives. The ICRC said they would do everything they could to help us and they kept their promise. It is undeniably true that our relationship with the ICRC maintained us through the long years to come.

19

Selvaratnam said the peace negotiations were a nonsense. But he took us to meet the delegation on their second visit to the North. I think it was in early 1995; we had been in captivity about six months by now. The Tigers had prepared for the nego-tiations in style—a house in Nallur or somewhere like that had been newly refurbished for the talks. Motorcycle outriders were provided to the visiting delegation.

Selvaratnam drove me and Vijitha to have lunch with the del-egation. By this point, I was already so habituated to being a prisoner that I waited for a command to get out of the jeep. Selvaratnam said 'go, go, go!' He didn't come inside. But I still felt absent during the meeting. I was a prisoner now. I couldn't suddenly shift back to being a naval officer.

Whatever Selvaratnam had said I believe there was some hope for these peace talks at the time. The new President, Chandrika Bandaranaike Kumaratunga, was very popular in the North. Her party had won the parliamentary elections some months earlier, pushing back into opposition the party that had presided over the entire military conflict to date. To mark that first election, the Tigers had actually made a commemorative gesture of freeing some policemen they had in custody. I had been at home at that time, watching their release on television with my wife—I remember we talked about how happy they must have been to see their families again.

At the lunch with the negotiating team, I was quiet and withdrawn. A naval colleague in the delegation had contacted my family and brought me a message from them. The President's Permanent Secretary told me that the President had asked him to bring back news of me. He assured me that the next time they came they would take us back with them. I knew this was unlikely but I still remember the line. I don't think they did one thing about it.

* * *

We carried on with our lives in captivity. Mohan was only ever kind to me. He and his family were Sai devotees and he was a god-fearing man who went to temple every day. He was a strict vegetarian. He would not drink tea, just plain milk. During my first week, Mohan brought me a book called *Sai Baba Avatar*, written by an Englishman. He also later gave me a photograph of Sai Baba and told me it would protect me. On the first birthday I spent in captivity, he brought me some holy ash. I still carry it in my wallet today.

Selvaratnam always brought me the English newspapers. He did this from the very beginning of my stay with him. Southern newspapers were still available. Even in Tiger controlled areas some civilian administration continued, carried out by the state, and so goods like these did arrive from the South. Often I would read my own story in the papers—both the stories that had been translated from the Tiger media as well as the stories that had been translated from pure speculation. This is how I learnt a Board of Enquiry had been convened in my absence. The attack on the *Sagarawardene* had been investigated by the Navy and I had been found guilty of negligence, for keeping my ship in one place; found guilty without my ever having told my side of the story. Selvaratnam discussed it with me and asked me questions about what would happen if I went back.

At ICRC meetings, I would always meet the LTTE translator, George Master—or George Uncle as we called him. He provided another friendly encounter that recurred through my captivity. By the time I knew him, he must have been in his 60s—a retired post-master who had served in Ratnapura and elsewhere around there, in the south of the island. He was fluent in all three languages—Tamil, Sinhala and English—and was the official LTTE translator. The ICRC had its own translators so he never actually translated for us. At the meetings I spoke in English, without a translator and the others spoke in Sinhala, either through the translator or through me. All the LTTE cadres were kept out of the room. But George Uncle was simply present around the place and would seek me out to talk to me.

He spoke mainly about the good times he had known in his career as a post-master and how sad he had been to leave all that. With the riots in 1983 he had been displaced. Almost overnight he had been pushed out of the life he was living and returned to his home town in the Vanni. His commitment to the movement was real but he was willing to concede there had been good times.

Even the guard Sridharan, after my first altercation with him, became friendlier. We knew our places, now. He would come to the window and chat to me while he was on duty. My Tamil was still minimal but it was enough for us to have a basic conversation. I asked him how he had lost a leg. It had been during the Trividabalaya operation, he said. This was a three force move by the Sri Lankan military to recapture Elephant Pass and open a passage for troop movements on land. Elephant Pass is the narrow corridor that links the northern Jaffna peninsula to the rest of the island of Sri Lanka. Sridharan had lost his leg in fire from a gunboat. Yet, he was not sorry; he was about 18 or 19 and waiting to get back to the front.

No one else took pity on him either—there just wasn't that *'aney pau'*[26] mentality. In the LTTE movement, stretched as it was, you were never useless until dead. Sometimes Sridharan would bathe at the well. He would do this by taking off his 'Jaipur leg' and seating himself on a chair. From this sitting position he could draw water from the well. While he was bathing, other cadres would come and confiscate his prosthetic leg, just for kicks. Mohan told me that at the front people climbed trees without legs. His voice was full of respect as he said it.

* * *

One night Selvaratnam and Mohan told us to pack our things. All we had, at this point, was a mat and a pillow each. Vijitha was worried again. As for myself, again I allowed myself to wonder if we were being released.

Instead this turned out to be the first of many moves. We were blindfolded and put in the back of the jeep.

They drove us away. We travelled for maybe an hour before we arrived at our destination and were told to get down. We were taken inside a house. Selvaratnam and Mohan followed with our mats and pillows. There had been shelling the night before, close to where we had been. I realised this was probably why we were moved. Maybe they thought the Sri Lankan Armed Forces had identified our location and were about to attempt a rescue.

We moved a few times with Selvaratnam. Once we were put in a hallway and told not to talk to each other. Another time, we were given two beds on a verandah. I learnt later that many of these locations had been around the area of Manipay, not far from Jaffna town. I'd already suspected that despite the long journeys between places, we'd stayed in one area. In a few different houses I'd heard the same dog barking, though each time at a different distance away.

This was also, I came to know, during a series of operations and counter operations between the Sri Lankan military and the LTTE. The Government's Operation Leap Forward was answered by Pulipachchal, meaning Tiger Jump. The Government then came back with their Riviresa operation. These were all attempts to secure control of the Peninsula. It felt as though power kept moving from one hand to the other. One morning Selvaratnam came and told us we were moving again. The blindfolds were put on. When they were removed again we were in a highly fortified cell. Selvaratnam was gone.

20

I felt some shock at our sudden removal from Selvaratnam's care. This was in July 1995, just over nine months since our capture. I knew this because just before we were moved our guards had celebrated Black Tiger Day, an LTTE anniversary commemorating their first successful suicide bombing. Selvaratnam had been there then. Now we were being watched by guards we hadn't seen before.

For the first few days, there wasn't a major change. But I had the sense that some period of grace was over. The Government's Riviresa operation was attacking with full force. Overhead, we could hear the wheezing of shells being launched from the camp at Palaly. They shot south over the town, towards the islands. This was what first gave me a sense of where in the town we were. Then we heard other voices. I remembered that when we'd met Jude, a friend of Mohan's, he'd talked about a Sinhala prisoner called Sampath. He said Sampath was at Nallur, with the rest of the Army guys. The chances were that this was where we had also now been brought, into the heart of Jaffna.

We were in a cell together here, Vijitha and I. High on one wall was a small barred fanlight that was our only window on to the outdoors. One day we saw a face at the window—a man had jumped up to its height and was gripping the bars to keep him-self up there. '*Army-tha?*' he asked us, 'Are you Army?' We only had time to say 'Navy' before he dropped down again.

We realised later that this man was the tallest of the other prisoners and the best able to perform this trick. A few days later he came again, with another guy. This time they asked '*Navey kattiyatha?*' 'Are you the guys from the ship?' We said we were. Two of these men would be let out of their cell each morning to pump water up to an overhead tank for all our use. They could only ask questions quickly as they passed the opening to our cell. They did not want anyone to see them speaking to us. They couldn't afford to be caught and lose the privilege of leaving their cell once a day.

Vijitha and I were new, and still cowed. We just answered their questions, never asked any of our own. Later we learnt that the Army boys had heard of our capture—mine specifically. The Sinhala books we had been given to read in Manipay had later been passed on to them. With this, Jude had told them of our existence. These prisoners had all been in custody longer than we had and were more accustomed to captivity. They would some-times try to reassure us: '*bayavenna epa*', 'don't be scared' they'd say. Of this crew, Sampath was the friendliest and best able to get around the guards. He was liked by Mudalvannan, our new jailer.

We were now under the overall charge of Pottu Amman, head of the LTTE's intelligence and suicide operations. But we never met him—Mudalvannan was the man we knew. Mudalvannan wasn't much of a talker—he only really spoke if we initiated conversation. I don't remember anything particular about his story. I think it was an ordinary tale of poverty that had led him to the movement—though his name meant 'money man'. We exchanged a few words here and there and became some com-pany to each other. I felt that these young cadres were also captives of a sort. Mudalvannan was serving a punishment turn on his way out of the movement. Sometimes LTTE cadres who wanted to leave did have their cases heard, on the basis of family circumstances and such like. If their resignation was approved they would still have to serve out a notice period in some of the less glorious jobs the movement had to offer. Being a jailer was one of these.

Mudalvannan must have been in his mid-twenties at this point; lean, tall and always smiling. At the Nallur house he was a one man show, looking after the Army guys as well as Vijitha and me. I have a feeling that Vijitha and I got some treats that the others did not, on account of there being only two of us. Mudalvannan, once he had served our meals, would bring his own food to eat at our door. Our food was different from his and sometimes he would offer us an extra curry from his lunch. Otherwise we just ate pittu and brinjals here and for some years after. We were real prisoners now.

We spent our days waiting for meals, just to punctuate the day. I think we had lunch at one or two and then dinner at about six-thirty, before the light faded. Since there was no electric light, after dinner we had nothing to do but to go to sleep. During the day I would read the books left over from the last ICRC visit, sometimes for the second or third time. The book I remember best was Nelson Mandela's *A Long Walk to Freedom*. This was an account that inspired me and helped me maintain perspective. Mandela had not been cowed by a much harder twenty-seven year captivity; I was determined to survive whatever was left of mine. I must have read the book three or four times over the course of my captivity—sometimes reaching the end and turning back to the beginning.

The ICRC was our link to the world. Beyond our meals, ICRC visits were the only thing we had to look forward to. I marked the days off on small calendars we were given at each visit. Mostly these were just things to do. It was a matter of living for the hour. If you survived this hour the next hour would be there for you. I think I learnt to do this instinctively—to find a way to exist in a permanent state of suspense. We had no autonomy even to go crazy.

The LTTE also kept us on the shortest possible leash. There were no routines. This was, I think, done deliberately, so that we could not try to plan an escape. Sometimes they gave us false information to confuse us—perhaps about an impending ICRC visit. I believe that the psychological pressure this put on us was also intentional. It was a constant reminder of who was in charge. Perhaps this is how you run a prison. Perhaps it's just human cruelty.

It was this power game, rather than our actual conditions, that reminded us we were prisoners. I think it is human instinct to acclimatise. After a while, the place you're in, whatever it is, starts to become home. We started to feel the food was good. It was only in the days immediately after an ICRC lunch that we'd find the meals back in our cell to be meagre and tasteless. At our ICRC visits we were spoken to as men rather than prisoners. But it was the LTTE who determined whether we could go to meet the ICRC. It was made clear to us—through their actions not their words—this was a treat rather than a right.

This prison had also once been a regular house. It was set back from the main road—I think on one of those by-lanes leading up to a plot of land. I wouldn't be able to recognise it from the outside. The strategy was to mix these military houses in with civilian houses for camouflage and protection. It was a normal Jaffna house, with a tiled roof, that had been modified into a jail. The house was divided into different cells off an intersection of two corridors.

Our cell was at the back of the house. Vijitha and I slept on the mats we had brought with us; the ones we had been sleeping on since our first night in Selvaratnam's custody. At the other end of the room was an open squatting toilet. We also bathed in this toilet area with a hose that was passed through the grill door. There was a hole in the floor through which the water could drain out afterwards. We could hear a bell—a husky far off sound which the guards later told us came from the Nallur temple.[27]

The greatest change in our circumstances after we arrived at the Nallur house was that we were put in chains. One of the things that the Army guys had asked us—in their passing whispers and notes thrown into our cell—was whether we were in chains. So we had some idea that might come. A single chain was brought for each of us. They were heavy chains—each link was about 1 inch in diameter. You know the chains—the ones used on elephants? Each end of the chain was passed around an ankle and padlocked to itself in a loop. So, in this way, our legs were chained together. The padlocks were there to act as clasps around each ankle. That was how it began. Then a few days later the padlocks were removed and the chain links actually welded together in the same position—making the chain very slightly lighter.

Each time we visited the ICRC, the chains were removed and then replaced when we returned. It could be a very painful process having the links welded back around our ankles. You could get electric shocks from the electric arc welder or you could get your feet burnt. Generally a stem of banana leaf was used as a buffer during the welding, placed between our ankles and the chain. This was some protection. But then water was poured over the chain to cool it down. That water absorbed the heat from the newly welded links and came down very hot on our feet. Eventually we learnt the trick: you had to turn your foot fast, away from the water as it came down. If you didn't you'd get a blister like a one rupee coin.

It takes a while to learn to walk in chains. You have to shuffle rather than walk. It also constricts the mind. Eventually, after years in chains, it took us some time to learn to walk without them.

21

Vijitha and I became cell-mates. At my release I joked that I had spent more nights with Vijitha than I had with my wife. This was probably true—I had been away from home for long spells throughout my marriage on account of being in the Navy. I had certainly never spent eight consecutive years at home as I did in captivity.

It was at the Nallur house that I first had a chance to talk to Vijitha. He had been in the Navy ten years—which would have put him in his early 30s. I was in my early 40s. Vijitha was recently married and had a young daughter, not yet one. I suppose it must have been while we were on the *Sagarawardene* that she was born. He must have taken leave for her birth but I don't remember it. Vijitha was from an area called Akurambada, near Matara on the southern coast. His father was alive and he had two older sisters who were not married. Vijitha's wife was a teacher, from the hill country. His father-in-law was a postmaster with some status in the village. Vijitha's marriage had been of his own choosing and he worried that he had done things out of turn to marry before his sisters were settled. He worried about his sisters a lot. He felt a responsibility for seeing that they were cared for.

Vijitha had been my Leading Supply Assistant on board the *Sagarawardene*. This was the first time he had served with me. On board the ship, crew management was handled by the Executive Officer, my second in command, so I had had no reason to speak with Vijitha. Still, we were not meeting as strangers when we started to share a cell. We had spoken at ICRC visits and, most importantly, shared nearly a year of captivity by this point.

Vijitha was no great talker anyway. But he was a great worrier. The pattern of our interaction was that he would fret and I would reassure him, each time promising that I would never leave him alone in captivity. After ICRC visits we would have more to talk about than on other days. We could share news from the letters we had received.

In later years, Vijitha and I would talk about the past. That is what you think about in captivity. Nothing is happening in the present and you can't let yourself think about the future. You have a lot of time and your life is not moving forwards. So you go back and reflect on the past. It is exactly the opposite of life outside the cell. There you are busy living in the present and planning for the future.

I thought a lot about my years growing up—in school and in the Navy. Mostly this was done in solitary reflection, but sometimes our thoughts would break through into conversation. Vijitha was fairly content in the Navy. He had joined after 1983 so he knew what he was getting into. Coming from Matara, he had witnessed the 1971 JVP insurrection and had Marxist sympathies. Yet he had joined the government forces. He hated the LTTE for capturing us. He refused to see what had happened in the context of their fighting a war. I also did not press him on that subject. I never myself felt that sort of animosity towards them. I honestly don't remember ever feeling that way. I only tried to say to Vijitha that there was nothing to be gained from feeling frustrated, since we could not change our situation.

Vijitha and I got to know each other well, naturally. He had gestures that signalled his thinking. He would stroke his moustache or lie down and fan his feet to and fro. When I saw his feet going I knew he was thinking deeply.

Vijitha would brush his teeth for what seemed like hours. I asked him why and he said he had to keep going until he got the taste of blood. When he used the toilet at all, he wanted to follow it with a full bath. He said these were old habits. Vijitha found it especially difficult at the start, when we were given a single bucket of water for everything. Insufficient water remained Vijitha's main complaint about our treatment. It led Mudalvannan to call us 'meen' or 'fish'.

I think these bathing rituals are cultural—Vijitha was used to bathing from a bottomless well. He was also a coastal man and counted on the proximity of water. I would tell him he was just pouring water away. Even the ICRC delegates asked if he was wasting water and that might be why he felt it so scarce? But Vijitha was a creature of strong habits. Since it was the Army guys who pumped the water for our use they would sometimes pump a little extra and tell us to enjoy a good bath. There was this feeling of solidarity, that we were all southern prisoners.

In general though, Vijitha was reserved, neither friendly nor unfriendly. So perhaps we never talked as much as you might imagine.

We were just four and a half months in Nallur but this house looms large in our experience because it was where we truly became prisoners. It was also our first encounter with the Army guys, though still only through brief exchanges at the fanlight. We met them again when we all had to leave Nallur, suddenly. This was our most dramatic departure.

We heard a lot of firing one morning and Vijitha and I wondered what it meant. Mudalvannan had told us the Army was trying to break out of its confines in Palaly. Day by day the shells had felt nearer, which had to mean the Army was getting closer to Jaffna town. Now even inside our cell we felt the shockwaves of wind that you get from an exploding shell.

An agitated Mudalvannan came and told us to pack. We could hear a truck arriving on the premises. All our cells were opened—I still remember the rattling noise of so many men scuttling in chains. We were dodging shells as we went. We were all loaded into the back of the truck. Mudalvannan got in too and we were off.

There was darkness inside the lorry but a mood of huge excitement. After all, we prisoners were all from the Sri Lankan forces and what we had just witnessed—and escaped—was their re-capture of the Jaffna peninsula. Despite our good relations with our jailers it was a sad day for them and a jubilant one for us, whilst all running for our lives.

This was two days before the LTTE ordered the civilian population to leave Jaffna town, giving them ten hours in which to do it, with the threat that after that time they would blow up the bridges over the lagoon.

LAND LOCK

22

We were fleeing the town that would soon be re-captured by Government forces. We would not be coming back in the years of captivity ahead, but rather moving gradually deeper into the jungle.

The camp at Kodikamam was set on a coconut estate. Away from urban areas the LTTE had to set up camp under tree cover, in order to conceal themselves from aerial bombing. Coconut trees don't do the job as well as jungle trees. But just outside a town—as Kodikamam is—they are the best you can get. The trees offered us better shelter too. We had more shade and cool air than we had known in Jaffna.

On this estate, our cells themselves were more restrictive. Where previously we'd been held in converted houses, here we were locked up in purpose-built prison cells. They were solid, concrete cells. A one man cell was about 10 feet by 3 feet. Initially, Vijitha and I were put in a one man cell together. Later, when a bigger room fell vacant, we were moved there. There were rows of adjacent cells. The walls were shared, but neighbouring cells opened in opposite directions. This way, prisoners could not speak to each other by coming to the grill doors to talk and be heard. But sometimes at Kodikamam we heard very faint voices. We couldn't tell where they were coming from and wondered if there were also underground cells.

The lucky thing at this camp was that because there was no water supply to the cells, we had to be taken out, to bathe at the well. We had been indoors for about eighteen months at this point. At last we could get a little fresh air and exercise. Mudalvannan was in charge again. He knew us by now and would indulge us if we asked to walk around a little, in our chains. We couldn't see beyond the property; just the trees of the estate and odd blocks of concrete prison cells built under their cover. Mudalvannan let us have a bath at least every other day and spend as long as we wanted at the well. Here there was enough water even for Vijitha. The food was also slightly better at Kodikamam. Because we were on a coconut estate, there was at least no shortage of coconuts.

One day while we were at the well, I caught sight of some other prisoners, in yellow sarongs. For a moment I thought the Tigers had captured some Buddhist monks. But then, seeing them closer up, I realised who they were. A few months before, in August 1995, the LTTE had captured a merchant ship, the *M.V. Irish Mona*, and taken its crew hostage. Two of the crew had served with me in the Navy. Jayatubanda and Loyola Fernando had both been Masters of Arms on ships I'd captained. They had later left the Navy and gone to work on merchant ships. They were shocked to see their former captain now in chains.

I knew this because they started to leave notes for us under a stone by the well. These civilian prisoners were free to move around the estate while waiting for their release to be negotiated with their ship's owner—probably through the payment of a ransom. We learnt later, they were sometimes even allowed to go to the local shops. Jayatubanda would find a way to hide notes near the well, before Vijitha and I were brought there to bathe. Mudalvannan was never far away so we had to retrieve the notes surreptitiously when he was not looking.

They were simply notes of sympathy; an effort to keep us going through our trials. There was one set of verses Jayatubanda wrote, in which he described his shock at seeing my altered state. He couldn't believe it was me he was seeing, so thin and without rank. I managed to keep the poem with me through all my years of captivity, although I misplaced it after coming home. When Jayatubanda and Loyola Fernando were released, they went to visit my family, to let them know they had seen me.

There are only two other things that I remember happening while we were at Kodikamam.

We met the Army prisoners properly. Up to this point we had always been taken to meet the ICRC separately. The LTTE had kept Vijitha and me separate from the other military prisoners. But now, I think because they were under more pressure on the battlefront, they consolidated their energies. They took us all together to meet the ICRC at Point Pedro, the northernmost point of the island.

I have a particular memory of this visit because it was here I tasted a cigarette after years. I had been a smoker when I was younger but had quit when I got married. Vijitha was also a non-smoker so although we had been offered cigarettes by the ICRC, we had always refused. Many of the Army guys were smokers and at the Point Pedro visit there were cigarettes everywhere. I also had one. It was a tiny pleasure in a dull run of days. The Army boys were so anxious to smoke by the time they got to an ICRC visit that they'd smoke almost a whole pack at once.

The Point Pedro visit was the first time we were able to talk to these other men freely and not through hurried whispers at the fanlight. Much later, Amerasinghe told me that the boys had rehearsed for a first meeting. They knew a senior officer was in captivity and had talked about how they should address me. They didn't want me to pull rank on them or put on airs. They were determined not to let me. You have to remember that soldiers are used to a different set up than sailors are. The Army was at the time a more hierarchical institution. Officers commanded from the rear and soldiers went out to battle ahead of them. In the Navy, there isn't that option. When you're at sea the whole crew must pull together to man a ship. So we lived by the ship's protocols at all other times too.

There had been much discussion. These soldiers were very young and full of anxious bluster. They had said they would not call me 'sir'. They'd show me we were all prisoners and equals and that I couldn't expect any deferential treatment. Amerasinghe and Sampath, who were a little older, had tried to calm the others. They told them that the Army required its members to show respect to rank and that they themselves intended to do that. The younger soldiers finally agreed they would see what I was like.

In the end it didn't really come up—we met on friendly terms at Point Pedro and the soldiers saw I did not want any unearned respect. Many of the LTTE cadres referred to me as 'sir' so that in fact became the norm.

What did we talk about at Point Pedro? Oh, the battles we had fought; where we had been captured. Many of these men had been captured in the attack on the Army camp at Pooneryn. When I heard that, I reminded them that I had in fact transferred some of them there on board a naval vessel. Vijitha remembered the coconuts. We generally kept coconuts in a cage on deck, where they were less likely to spoil. Quite a few had gone missing on that run to Pooneryn. There were also a few soldiers in the group who had been taken in another battle, near the Welioya camp. They had all heard of the attack on the *Sagarawardene*, while they were in captivity. They wanted to hear the story.

We exchanged a few notes on our conditions in LTTE captivity. To date, their experience had not been as good as ours. For the first few weeks, not only were their feet chained but their hands were also manacled behind their backs. During mealtimes their hands were tied in front and they'd do their best to shovel food into their mouths with bound hands. They were beaten—except for those who were spared because they were wounded. Conditions had improved since, but the Tigers did not treat them as worth much. It was different for me and, by proxy, Vijitha. The LTTE saw me as a potentially valuable chip with which to bargain in negotiations with the government. By declaring to the ICRC a prisoner well-treated, they also hoped to demonstrate to the world that they were a responsible self-governing authority. I was their show-prisoner.

The other thing that happened while we were at Kodikamam was that the Central Bank in Colombo was bombed by the LTTE. Mudalvannan brought our breakfast to us in an ecstatic mood. Mudalvannan was generally cheerful but today he was jubilant. We were starting to recognise these signs. We asked him what had happened. He said the 'biggest bank' in the South was gone. I thought immediately of my wife's first cousin who worked there. Mudalvannan made it sound like the whole of the Central Bank had been reduced to rubble.

Vijitha and I discussed it a little, after Mudalvannan left. The Central Bank was after all the nerve centre of the economy. In the weeks that followed, I worried that my family may have lost a close relative in the blast. With time to think, I remembered that my wife had jewellery in a safety deposit box at the Central Bank. I wondered if that would also have gone.

I worried that this incident would impact our chances of release. Everything that happened to sour relations between the Government and the LTTE had an impact on us too. I knew that typically when a ceasefire collapses, a war intensifies. It would be a new Eelam war for the Tigers. On a day to day basis, however, we lived with this irony: if our own side was doing badly, our treatment as prisoners improved. When our jailers were happy they treated us better. Sometimes when our own forces were struggling, we would get treats at mealtimes.

The next ICRC visit did not come for another month and a half. It was only when we did have this next meeting that I learnt from my wife's letters that her cousin was safe. We also got to read southern newspaper reports of the attack. This was one of the most successful and symbolically significant attacks the Tigers ever made on the South—in early 1996. We had already seen a few pictures in LTTE papers that had been brought to us, but those didn't carry lists of casualties.

By this time we had moved locations again, a little further down the road, to Mirusuvil.

Mirusuvil was another coconut estate. This time we were brought into it without blindfolds. The set-up was much the same as at Kodikamam—here was another purpose-built prison camp. We were in a corner cell again. This time there was a water supply to the cell, so we didn't get to go out. Any exercise we wanted had to be taken inside the cell. I was losing weight and my eyes were weakening. I would go to the door of the cell and try to focus on any object at a distance, usually the sky. If I didn't make this effort I would only ever be focusing on objects close at hand. The muscles of my eyes were consistently tensed.

Our stay in Mirusuvil was the shortest yet. We were there just over a month. The LTTE were on the run. We guessed that Government forces were attempting to re-capture Elephant Pass. They must have been getting closer. We knew that re-capturing the peninsula would be a huge boost to the military. It would also be a huge a symbolic loss to the LTTE, to lose the capital of Tamil Eelam. This time we were cheerful, while Mudalvannan looked worried. What this would mean for us as prisoners was a little murkier. For the Government to drive the Tigers back into the jungles was also to push them away from negotiation. We were getting pushed away with them.

23

Mudalvannan told us one evening to get ready for another move. We rolled up our mats and waited. As usual, Vijitha wondered if this next journey would be the one to our deaths. We were brought dinner. It may have been about eight o'clock when we heard a vehicle approaching. We heard the iron gates of the compound being opened and closed. Mudalvannan came to unlock our cell and we were escorted to a bus. When we got in we saw that the Army guys were already seated inside. We set off.

We weren't blindfolded this time but we couldn't see where we were going, in the darkness. Then we started to smell the sea. The bus stopped and we were told to get down. We were on some sort of beach.

We were herded into a boat; it was a big boat meant for carrying people. We could see fishing vessels in the distance. Once the boat started to move I knew we must be on the Kilali lagoon. The water was too calm for it to be the sea.

An alarm bell went off inside me. With civilian movement prohibited, I knew the Navy patrolled Kilali crossings and I knew they had no mercy at night. In the distance, we could see the lights of the Army and Navy bases. Because everything else was dark, they gave off a glow. But nothing happened. I looked up and followed the celestial bodies from east to west, by which I knew we were heading south. It was growing light by the time we reached the bank. There was a lorry parked there and we were all loaded into it.

Here began a journey I will never forget. You have to remember the roads in these parts were not tarred or maintained. We were twenty-two men in the back of a lorry. It was a regular lorry—the ones we use for transporting goods—but with full doors at the back rather than half doors. This was the dry season. We travelled for hours, dust from the outside seeping in through the closed doors of the vehicle. Inside it felt like a sandstorm. There was almost no visibility. We arranged ourselves on our bundles and did our best to endure the incessant bumping of the truck along the road. I suppose Mudalvannan was up front, in the driver's cab.

We stopped somewhere, probably by another LTTE camp. All we could see when they opened the doors was the barren spread of the Mannar landscape. We were given tea and a biscuit in the back of the truck. This happened twice, I think. No, there were no stops for toilets. You have to remember that we were quite a conspicuous crew. We were wearing chains and speaking Sinhala. The Tigers would not have wanted to risk any civilians seeing us and informing the authorities of our whereabouts.

We carried on for—I don't know—four or five or six hours. It was completely dark inside. Finally, we stopped. We were told to get out of the truck. Covered in dust from head to foot, we were like camouflaged men. You could run a finger over us and draw a line.

We were led to a well and allowed to have a much wanted bath. It was about lunchtime now. We were kept outside while we waited for lunch to be cooked. Even after lunch, we were allowed to stay outside until evening. Soon we were to realise why. One of the more senior cadres, who had accompanied us on this journey, finally came to get us. He ushered us all into a single cell and began to padlock the gate.

We started to protest wildly—shocked by this new development—but he clicked the padlock shut and walked away. Here was real fear. Was this the way it was going to be, now? The cell was about 10 feet by 10 feet. There was just enough space for twenty two men if we remained standing, or squatted on one spot. Eventually we worked out a way to rotate our positions so that each of us had some time leaning against a wall. That way everyone we could get a little sleep each night. We asked each other what this was all about. It was April, the hottest month of the year.

On the morning of the third day someone came and started pointing and selecting. Ten men were left in this cell. The rest of us were parcelled out into smaller cells. It was only some days later that we heard what had happened. They had forgotten to bring padlocks. The only padlock the guards had with them was the one that had secured the back of the truck. So, we had to be kept in a single cell until more padlocks could be procured.

Now Vijitha and I were in one cell, sharing it with someone else for the first time. Amerasinghe was the third and gave us new conversation. He was from the Ceylon Light Infantry. The battle at Pooneryn was led, on the Army's side, by the Gajaba regiment and the CLI. Amerasinghe had taken a shot to the arm in this battle and begun to lose a lot of blood. The Tigers spotted and captured him.

Ours was a one man cell and small for three. To sleep we arranged ourselves next to each other, head to toe. Two men got to sleep with their heads away from the toilet; one man with his head inevitably pointing towards it. Vijitha was not much of a talker, so Amerasinghe generally spoke more with me. Amerasinghe was from Piliyandala, just outside Colombo. His wife was also a soldier, in the Army medical corps and the regular women's battalion. He was a Catholic; she was a Buddhist. Of the Army prisoners in fact only Amerasinghe and Nomis were married. Hemapala, the eldest, was not married and the other soldiers were very young. We talked a lot about Amerasinghe's career. He was a corporal and had been in the Army about ten years. He must have been in his early 30s when I knew him. He was calm in general but a hothead when he got worked up.

What I remember most of this place—near Periyamadu—was the impossible April heat. Heat was the most powerful form of weather we experienced anywhere. Three men in a 3x10 foot cell are always close enough to feel each other's heat. Sometimes we would take off our vests, squeeze the sweat out of them and put them on again. You could wring about a half cup of sweat from each vest.

Amerasinghe couldn't wash his own clothes on account of his injured hand so I said I would wash them for him. He was hesitant at first. He felt it was asking an indignity of a higher ranking officer. I told him not to be silly—how else were we going to do it?

We were in slightly weaker health by now. There was no exercise to be had and the meals were very frugal. We started to lose a lot of weight. My sight was weakening, with age, poor light, too much reading and too little other use. We caught malaria, though the ICRC was medicating us against it. The LTTE called it 'jungle fever'. It was really the only thing we came down with in captivity—we were not exposed to other human beings from whom we could catch infections. But LTTE paramedics came to see us every day. Yes, every day, in every place we were held. And if we called for them, they always came. They would administer quinine for malaria. They could recognise it from the shivers and severe headaches and losses of appetite. Since Manipay, we hadn't visited a hospital. Mentally? I think we were ok. When you don't have alternatives you adapt fast. The mind and body adjust themselves to restriction, I believe. Your mind stays in, in a sense.

Perhaps life at sea had helped to prepare me for this time—even before I became a prisoner, I was used to restrictions being placed on food, water and space. When new constraints were imposed, Vijitha complained about them and then eventually had to accept them. I knew we would have to accept anything thrown at us, so I did not bridle against my circumstances. I think this helped me. Sure, sometimes it was a strain keeping Vijitha's spirits up. But I think I also used it as a tactic to keep myself strong. It meant I kept reinforcing the positive for myself, as much as for him. I think these strategies for survival exist in all of us; it's just that they are not usually tested.

You ask what kept me going? My upbringing and my naval training were the things that I drew on. My parents were people of strong, stoic principles and growing up we had been encouraged to be self-sufficient and to face life without complaint. Naval training had given me discipline. I didn't want to die so I had to live. I wanted to live. I wanted to leave. There was some hope, so I went on that. You try to face each hour in the best spirits you can muster. Then, as I said, the next hour is there for you. To think about a whole day at a time is too much like thinking about the future. An hour is manageable, repeatable.

Overall, I measured time in ICRC visits and we were in Periyamadu for about four. This could have been a whole year. We had stopped running. This was another coconut estate, but in the interior of the Vanni,[28] protected by jungle. Until the Army started moving this way, we could stay.

24

One day we were told we had a visitor. We were taken outside and assembled in a circle under a tree. Here, Karikalan came to speak to us. He was then a leader in the LTTE political wing. He said perhaps we could assist in securing our own release. He suggested that we write to the Leader of the Opposition, and ask him to press the Government to send a representative to negotiate for the release of their prisoners. I can't remember the exact conversation but this was the gist of it.

If we could get the ball rolling, they were prepared to negotiate with the Government, he said. They would be willing to exchange the twenty-two of us for three LTTE cadres in Government custody. He asked if we would write, to see if we could get the process started. We were willing. We had not seen any moves to negotiate our release. We could only imagine being released if there was a peace settlement. We agreed to write letters.

These were sent to the then Leader of the Opposition, Ranil Wickremesinghe, through the ICRC. The matter was subsequently raised in Parliament. The response from the President was apparently that she didn't know such a group was being held. The Defence Secretary is said to have said that the Government considered prisoners as dead soldiers. The bookseller Vijitha Yapa, however, contacted the ICRC and through them sent me complimentary subscriptions to *Newsweek* and *National Geographic*.

I suppose it should not have been a great surprise that the Government response was indifferent, even callous. Military forces are designed precisely to make every soldier replaceable. Go and ask a decommissioned soldier, anywhere in the world, how he is being looked after now. Look at statistics for criminal activities being committed by former or serving soldiers. Ask a prisoner what it's like to be told his government doesn't plan to do anything for his release. The Sri Lankan Government was sending a signal that they did not want to do business with the LTTE in any way. Eventually the three LTTE cadres in Government custody were released by the courts, since they could not legally be held any longer.

It was while we were at Periyamadu the Mullaitivu debacle took place. As usual our jailers looked happy and told us the story. The Tigers had cornered and completely destroyed the Government's military camp at Mullaitivu, capturing the town. Around 1200 Government troops were killed. As ever, when something good happened for their side, the Tigers were ever ready to talk. When they sustained losses they would be moody and monosyllabic. There was one of those times at Periyamadu, too. The LTTE had planned to attack the Welioya camp but the Army received early information of their plans. The Army lured the attackers into the camp and then came down on them with all their force—I think two or three hundred female cadres were killed.

In bad times for the LTTE our treatment worsened. They needed a way to show their displeasure and their resources also got squeezed. Food would be late and poor. There was extra security and our jailers were unhappy and short with us. Sometimes we would not learn what had given rise to such a change until we got to our next ICRC visit and read the newspapers from months before.

But in general, the guards were now a friendlier part of our lives. And we ourselves were becoming a group. I had a new responsibility, of leading the group, as the eldest and a senior officer. I felt I'd almost taken on a job. I now had work. It kept my mind occupied. Occasionally it was aggravating but I think it was good for me overall. That was a significant change that took place for me around this time.

I mean, I still did not have regular contact with the whole group, except at ICRC visits. But sometimes in this place we could listen to the chatting from neighbouring cells. If no one was around to stop us, we talked across cells. By this point I think the guards trusted us. But they would still routinely inspect our cells. It was apparently to guard against arson. I think, more than that, it was to remind us we were prisoners.

There were some familiar cadres. Kapilan was in charge but he rarely visited. We felt more of an abandoned group by now—a long way from Selvaratnam's daily visits. Some of our guards were young boys, I imagine not even eighteen yet. They had some confidence in us and we in them. But there was always an armed guard at our door. You could never completely forget you were a prisoner. Mudalvannan seemed to be a fixture of our lives and then at some point he disappeared. I wondered if he had finally earned his release.

You seem surprised that the LTTE had such an extensive network of prisons. I think these were mostly for their own traitors—cadres who were in trouble with the movement, paramilitaries from rival groups, disobedient civilians. In the extreme corner of our block was a big man in a cell of his own, who had to me the look of a movement leader. I had asked who he was but I don't think anyone ever told me. To this day I think he was a leader imprisoned on some suspicion. Then, one day, he was no longer there.

Another thing that happened while we were at Periyamadu was that Sri Lanka won the Cricket World Cup. We knew Sri Lanka had made it to the final because the guards had come to tell us. They were excited too. Even the LTTE made an exception for cricket. They would not call it the Sri Lankan team— they never used the new name of the country—but they supported it. They were big fans of Sanath Jayasuriya and Arjuna Ranatunga. It was a source of great pride to them that a Tamil player, Muttiah Muralitharan, should be one of the new stars of the team.

On the day of the final, the guards on duty made a point of frequently coming to our cell doors. By doing this, they could allow us also to catch the commentary on the pocket radios they carried. They'd come and update us on the score. You ask me if I remember any moments from the match? Not really; we didn't hear enough for that. But it was still one of our most exciting days in captivity. Sri Lanka had never been in a World Cup final before. Most of us were cricketers ourselves. When Sri Lanka won, the guards cheered with us.

But mostly days just passed. That's how it was. Then, one day they would come and say—get ready, come out, get into a truck. They'd drive you away. Then you'd know you'd left.

25

This time it was the Government's Edibala operation, coming up along the Madhu Road, that forced us to move. But we didn't go far. We went a little further inland to Mundumurippu, just out of artillery range. There were no blindfolds anymore. We were in the jungles of the Vanni—an area too vast and unmarked for us to track our way out of it. I think the Tigers also felt by then that we were just another part of their outfit. Where the cadres went, we went. I expect it was a burden on the LTTE to have to keep these twenty-two declared prisoners safe. But they still wanted to prove their worth to the international community. Besides, the deed was done. They had declared us to the ICRC. Now they were compelled to look after us.

We were now in bigger cells, under a thicker canopy of mahogany and *palu* trees. We found a few names scratched into the cell wall, in Sinhala, along with military service numbers. This was our first actual indication since capture that there had been prisoners before us. We did not know what had happened to them—and they hadn't risked any more than their names on the walls.

One day, a man called Sangeethan came to see me, with a translator. He asked how I liked my living conditions. I said I was ok. He said I could be given better accommodation. I refused politely; I said I was happy to stay where I was. I did not want to be alone and I did not want the other men to lose their leader. I felt the job I was doing was helping. It helped to keep them going and it helped me to keep going.

About a week later I was sent for. I was taken to a room in another building. Sangeethan was here again, with a translator. He asked me about my family. He wondered how my children were growing up. He said they could arrange for me to return to my family. They would release me and I could choose a few of the others to go with me. There was something they would ask of me in return, he said. They wanted me to find shelter for LTTE cadres crossing into the South to gather intelligence. It would be my job to house and find plausible cover for them. I didn't have to gather information myself, just keep the information gatherers safe. They would cover the costs of this. I would, myself, be a paid LTTE operative serving this function.

I was not tempted. I had endured three years in captivity; I knew I could survive here. I was prepared to hold out for a real release—which these terms were not. I knew enough of the LTTE to be sure that I would not be able to default on the promise once I'd made it home. To attempt that would mean certain death. To accept their offer would have been to go back on the conditions of service to which I had given my whole adult life to date.

But I was scared. I did not know if they would allow me to refuse an offer like this. I tried to say, as politely as possible: 'it's a difficult task you would be setting me, which I may not be able to fulfil. So, better I stay here'. I was careful not to make any political objection. Rather, I suggested I was worried about my family. Sangeethan was calm—he didn't press the matter. He said 'the decision is yours'. He said there were a lot of people in the South helping them and I shouldn't miss the opportunity of going home.

I went back to my cell, somewhat shaken. Naturally the others had seen me being led away; now they wanted to know what had transpired. I gave vague answers. I said they had asked questions about how we were all doing. I never even told Vijitha the truth. I simply waited to see if anything bad would happen. Nothing did. There was no change in my conditions. They did not come to check if I'd changed my mind. In truth, I don't think they could have been surprised—they knew me by this point.

By the time we had moved to Mundumurippu, the Tigers were under pressure and suffering on account of Government embargoes. What this meant to us was that the food was less and less good. So, we asked the ICRC if they would send us milk powder and sugar to go in our tea. Then we asked for biscuits. The guards benefited from these requests, since we naturally shared our supplies with them. We also persuaded the ICRC and the LTTE to let us take cigarettes back to the prison with us, suggesting that it would be better for our health than chain-smoking through ICRC meetings. That is the other thing I remember changing at Mundumurippu.

The guards still kept the cigarette stocks. After meals they would come and distribute a cigarette to each of us. But eventually they let us keep the cigarettes inside the cell. They were not allowed to smoke and did not want to be tempted. From then on, they just rationed our smoking by order. We were given matches. You look surprised? There isn't a lot you can do with a box of matches inside an empty concrete cell.

At each ICRC visit we would also be given something for which we hadn't asked. It might be a towel or a t-shirt or something like that. The role the ICRC really played for us was a psychological one. Even as this war dragged on, we knew we had been accounted for.

Even the guards were tired of the conflict and waiting for it to end. They chatted to us although they were supposed to stay aloof. Remember, these were not the LTTE's most dedicated members—these were the ones who wanted to leave. I always think one of the things that must have been hardest for the LTTE was to weather the natural changes in their cadres as they grew up. Many of the cadres we met had joined the movement as impassioned young boys. Credulous young men. Imagine—if you joined the movement at eighteen, ten years later you'd be twenty-eight, a completely different creature. You'd want a different sort of life by then—a family life. The struggle would no longer be everything. Besides you'd have been struggling with it some time. Where they could, many cadres escaped south and disappeared.

We never contemplated an escape. If we'd managed to get out of the camp we would still have been nowhere. We wouldn't have known where we were and wouldn't have known where to go, without help from LTTE insiders. If anyone had spotted us they would have known we were Sinhalese, even without our chains.

JUNGLE

26

By now, it was August 1997 and we had been nearly three years in captivity. As usual, one night we were suddenly asked to get ready. We piled into a bus and were driven off. We travelled for a few hours in the dark but then we stopped. They told us we were returning and brought us back to the cells we'd just left.

We learnt later that the LTTE was trying to move us north-west. But the very same night an Army recce unit had made a sudden move, infiltrating Tiger territory and crossing the path we would take. I wonder what would have happened if the LTTE had not received information of this move and we had run into them. We returned to Mundumurippu and spent about a month there. But then, as the Government's Jayasikuru Operation inten-sified, we were moved across the country to the jungles near Mullaitivu. Although we didn't know it at the time, this would be our last move with the LTTE. For three years we had been on the run, trying to stay ahead of military operations. Now we would spend five years in one jungle camp.

The final journey we made during the day. It was a two to three hour journey, finally turning on to a stretch of bad road that took us into the jungle. When we got down from the bus we saw a lot of activity. We saw many people moving about—

some others also in chains. Here the trees grew tall and there was a vast canopy that spread over us. The undergrowth had been cleared and a camp was being built.

We were first put in a temporary cage. We had been rushed into the move by Army operations and our cells had yet to be built. What they had ready was a standard issue animal cage that could easily be set up and dismantled. All twenty-two of us occupied a single cage. The floor area of the cage must have been about 20 feet by 20 feet. We could stand up inside it—the top of the cage was about two feet above my head. There were gates that could be opened and padlocked shut. I think we spent something like a month in that space. I'm not really sure.

In the mornings, before sunrise, they would take us out on a kind of jungle march. We'd each carry a mammoty[29] and a bucket of water. We'd dig our own toilets each day. I remember the dawn light in which we would carry out our 'farming sessions', as we called them. After we used our toilets we would cover them with earth. Then we'd come back to brush our teeth at another bucket of water. About twice a week we were allowed to bathe, with water from a new well that had been dug at the camp.

I think they probably just arrested masons when they needed them. They were constructing a very solid camp here—one of their last bastions—at Vallipuram near Puthukkudiyiruppu, I later learned. Someone told me that this camp was mentioned in the reporting from the battlefront at the end of the war. He said it must have been the place because there had been some mention of our captivity; the report had said 'this is where Boyagoda was held'. But I didn't hear it myself and it may not even have been the place.

It wasn't a large area that we used. Not only were our movements restricted by order but there were also landmines around. Apart from our morning excursions, we spent the rest of our time in our cell. That was where we took our meals. That was where we passed the time. If we wanted the toilet again, we had to have the guard's permission to go out. We dreaded attacks of diarrhoea.

Rain started to play a part in our lives now. When we were held indoors it had never really affected us. In fact, we would welcome the rain because it cooled the air. And sometimes we were allowed extra water to bathe in, because the wells were full. But I remember the rains were in progress when we arrived at this new jungle camp. The only protection we had was a tarpaulin thrown over the top of our cage. Powerful rains would still come in through the sides. Digging toilets could be a muddy business. Luckily, there were no leeches in this part of the country.

We were now placed in the hands of Sangeethan, the man who had carried the proposal to me about working for the LTTE. Sangeethan was not like most of our other guards. He hated us for being Sinhala, which was our first disadvantage. He was always looking to find fault with our behaviour. He invented transgressions as an excuse to punish us. And we could not trust that what he said would be what he did.

We had been lucky not to have guards like this before. Now we had to exist in a state of anxiety, and very often hunger. Sometimes the ration brought to us would be the weakest form of rice kanji: that is to say, the excess water in which other rice had been boiled. Our welfare was never of any concern to Sangeethan; his project was rather to keep us down. There was less food, less water, no changes of clothes. We had routinely to empty our cells and give up things we had been collecting.

I tried to make complaints on behalf of us all. I would tell the guards just outside our cage that I needed to speak with Sangeethan—the man in charge. Sangeethan ignored the messages. He sent new chains. I had always had two chains on each leg, while everyone else had one on each. Sangeethan now added an extra pair of chains for each of my fellow prisoners.

Sometimes, looking out of our cage, we'd see other chained groups being taken on a jungle march. So, we knew there were more prisoners. We suspected that traitors to the Tiger cause—both civilians and Tiger cadres—were the labour used to build the camp. It was some relief to see other people but it also fed my disgust. We saw the way that others had been treated. There were people who seemed only half-conscious, as though they were sleep-walking. I felt they must have been tortured. I have seen the torture chairs they locked people into, before starting to remove their fingernails. I never saw these things being done but we heard cries and sat in our cell, imagining. It came to a point where we told the ICRC that just hearing these screams felt like torture to us too. We asked to be moved away from the noises. After a time, it stopped. I don't think it was long before prisoners like that were finished with a shot to the head or a lamppost killing.

By this point we were fairly confident that we would not be subjected to torture, ourselves, apart from the slow suspense of captivity. That had become a way of life. It could feel normal if we accepted it without frustration. Frustration was the enemy to avoid, since there was nothing here to alleviate it.

I had never been a temple-going man. But, with time to myself, I learnt to meditate. From the time we were put in chains at Nallur, I realised life was going to get much harder. To prepare for that, I began to meditate. My wife and my mother-in-law would send Buddhist writings to me through the ICRC. I would meditate and chant *seth pirith*[30] in low tones. It would give me some relief. Buddhism is a very inward religion. To invoke its spirit felt like a release from my outward life in which I was being controlled by someone else. These are not things I knew until I had some need for them.

I don't actually know how long we spent in that cage: it could have been as little as a month or as much as six months. It was being together like this that turned us into one group. In

Periyamadu, while Amerasinghe was sharing a cell with Vijitha and me, he had told me a little about each of the other Army guys. He had told me that many of them were boys, just through their basic training, and asked me to excuse any immaturity in them.

Of course there was a lot of conflict, with that many young men closely confined together. In a situation like the one we were in, you simply cannot have things the way you want them. All you can do is select a common way of doing things and stick to it. Differences, arguments and fights usually escalated from one tiny thing or another. When we were all brought into a common cell, my being a senior officer had some impact on cooling their behaviour. What I had to do in turn was give them confidence I would be their true representative to the LTTE.

27

We complained to the ICRC about Sangeethan. We had been living under him for some months—maybe six or seven—and we were worried. What if his regime became the new norm? Perhaps eventually we would be beaten down like the other prisoners we had seen. I know that the things we experienced with Sangeethan are not unusual for prisoners to face. But in the previous three years we had seen nothing like it.

I knew we were show prisoners. The LTTE had not expected to capture me. When they did, they decided to use me to gain as much political mileage as they could. Their strategy to use me in bargaining with the Sri Lankan Government had hardly been very successful but the Tigers were still able to exploit me in their propaganda. They could show their supporters they had carried out a successful attack and taken a ranking prisoner. They could pretend to the international community that they were a responsible authority that abided by the nobler laws of war. The ICRC knew this, I expect—as did I. So we used it, too—to try to hold the LTTE to the high account of which they seemed to be boasting.

Within our first year at Puthukkudiyiruppu, Sangeethan was transferred. A new jailer, Newton, was brought in. Newton came to be a universal favourite—the best keeper of our captivity.

After we were moved into a permanent building, we were made an offer that we might work during the day. As prisoners under ICRC protection, unlike the other prisoners in the camp, we couldn't be forced by the LTTE to do anything. But many of us volunteered to help dig wells. It was a chance to get out of our cells and do something. We also had an incentive to work hard because we were digging a well for our own use. We made an effort to dig deep and get at good water, so we would never run short. We went down some 30 or 40 feet, finally lifting men into the well to fill up buckets of earth that we could draw out on a pulley. Once you hit water, that's when you line the sides of the well with rubble and wait for it to fill.

We worked from early in the morning until about lunchtime and then again in the late afternoon. Most of us joined in, glad of the exercise, but my younger companions spared me the heaviest tasks. Vijitha never came out; he preferred to sit in one place. Amerasinghe's hand was injured, so he couldn't help. Rambanda had wounds on his torso where a piece of shrapnel had passed right through his body. His arm didn't work properly anymore and he could not help either.

Hemapala also chose not to. Hemapala was the eldest among us, in his 40s, like me. He was a civilian cook for the Army and had been captured with the other soldiers. He was growing old in captivity and said he didn't need much more of life; if he could have a good smoke and die, he would be content.

But Sampath, for example, was always the very first to volunteer for anything. Ratnapala and Gamini were not far behind. Sisira and Nomis were also among the workers, as was Rupasinghe, on and off. We worked with our chains on—but we were never forced to work.

While we laboured, an armed guard kept watch. We'd been with the LTTE for years and I think by now they were confident we wouldn't try to run away. But they did not take the risk.

We were now receiving a lot more from the ICRC, as we thought of little ways to improve our lot. We asked for chilli powder. We were served hot kanji in the mornings and we found that adding chilli powder would improve the taste. Sometimes we were more ambitious and made a *katta sambol* paste out of chilli and oil, within our cell. We lit a piece of paper on fire and held it to the mix to cook it a little.

When we had originally complained to the ICRC about the food we received, they had offered to send dry rations for the prisoners. But of course many of these things did not come back to us from the LTTE kitchen. We told our new jailer, Newton, about the problem. He arranged for us to cook for ourselves. They put up a kitchen hut near our cell and after a few deliveries of flour and other materials from the ICRC we were ready to begin cooking. A ration of rice was sent to us from the LTTE kitchen, along with coconut and fresh vegetables.

From this point, we managed all our meals ourselves. We put up a roster outside the kitchen. Each day two of our number would make breakfast, lunch and dinner while the others went to work. This meant that each man did a turn in the kitchen every eleven days. We would make our own morning tea and roti for breakfast and keep going from there. It took some detailed care from Newton to set us up with everything we needed, over the course of perhaps a year.

Newton was a special person—the most humane of all my jailers. On the day he arrived, he came over to chat with me. He could speak a little English. From the first I knew he would be different. Sure enough, Newton heralded a gradual easing of our restrictions. The ICRC had requested that we be allowed to spend a couple of hours outside the cell each morning, even when we were not working. This was granted and gradually those few hours turned into whole days.

Newton let us create a makeshift cricket pitch. We played in our sarongs and chains, holding the chain up with one hand to shuffle faster down the pitch. Every evening at about four o'clock, Newton would come and let us out to play. He would join us himself and afterwards we'd invite him to have a drink with us. By now we were getting extra rations that included fruit cordials.

We could all speak reasonable Tamil by this point. When I joined the Navy I only had a 'vanakkam'[31] kind of Tamil. I picked up a little bit from the friends I made in the North but my speaking was still poor. It was on Karainagar, doing the work of civilian administration, that I suddenly needed a lot more spoken Tamil. I spoke in Sinhala to the people who spoke Sinhala but of course there were many who did not. So I would try out the Tamil I knew—never grammatical but gradually competent enough to get a message across.

The others were younger and had spent less time in the North than I had, so they had less spoken Tamil. But eventually everyone had enough to hold a basic conversation. In captivity, I spoke to Selvaratnam in English and to Newton in a mixture of English and Tamil. I spoke to Mohan and Ananda in Sinhala but otherwise we operated in Tamil. I've lost some of my Tamil since I came back to the South, but I can still hold a conversation.

28

We had about a year with Newton, in these better conditions. Then, all of a sudden, Newton was transferred and Sangeethan came back. Sangeethan could not or did not rescind all our privileges at once. But gradually, under one pretext or another, he shut down each of our liberties. The kitchen went; the recreation went. The reason given was that we had been plotting an escape. We had not been. Our circumstances were made difficult again and the constraints felt much harder after our period of liberty.

There were other things going on in the camp that may have explained the tightening of screws. A few months before, an Army deserter trying to escape through the jungle had blundered into our camp. Falling into Tiger hands he had surrendered to them. His surrender was accepted. He was treated better than a captive, acting as a mess-man to the guards and working in the kitchen. We weren't told any of this but we had seen this guy—who to us looked Sinhalese—moving around the camp.

One day the man came and beckoned to us—one of our number followed him into the forest and that is how we learnt his story. He said 'I am doing all this but I'm going to get these people'. It could have been bravado to play this line to us but I was suspicious of him. I told the others to be careful too.

All of this happened during Newton's time, when we were pretty content. We did not think much about this man but went about our own business. For the Sri Lankan New Year,[32] we made kiribath.[33] It felt good to furnish a celebration from our own kitchen. For Vesak,[34] we told Newton we wanted to make paper lanterns and he got us the sticks and coloured tissue and glue that we needed. We were outside one day, giving our yellow and white lanterns their final touches before Vesak, when we heard the sound of a blast. I immediately thought of the deserter.

The guards rushed over and blew their whistles. We were all put back in our cells. The next day we heard what had happened. The Army deserter had detonated a grenade during lunch, killing himself and injuring a few of the guards. He was of troubled mind, I think.

It was after this that Sangeethan was brought back. We suspected Newton had been transferred because he was feared to be too lenient. Even we were amazed that the LTTE would have taken such risks with a Sri Lankan Army deserter.

When our kitchen activity came to an abrupt halt we had to tell the ICRC to stop bringing us extra rations. We were back to milk powder, sugar, chilli powder and cigarettes. ICRC visits were now held at the LTTE political office in Puthukkudiyiruppu town; what they called their Muhilan base.

One of our saddest visits to the ICRC was to hand over the body of Hemapala, the only one of us to die in custody.

I had first got to know Hemapala when I shared a cell with him and Sampath and Vijitha in Mundumurippu. Hemapala and Sampath didn't click as personalities. Those two had a way of setting each other off. Did I tell you about the time when Hemapala and Sampath had a fight over a bar of soap? In that cell we had to take our baths inside. One day, Hemapala used Sampath's soap and Sampath complained. Sampath grumbled that at least Hemapala could have washed it after he used it. He took the bar of soap and started scrubbing it against another bar of soap. A tussle began—this time a physical fight. Vijitha and I had to step in to pull the two men apart. Try getting a firm grip on angry naked men, covered in soap! But in general Hemapala was a quiet character: a loner who never left the cell unless he had to.

One night in the jungle camp, I heard some commotion and calls for the paramedic. By now we were in two cells, half of our number in each. Hemapala was not in my cell but the other one; we could only hear the commotion. Later, I was told that he had smoked two cigarettes before he went to sleep that night. He offered another to Rupasinghe. At one point in the night, he had got up and squatted on his haunches. He put his head down as if in resignation and told another prisoner he was not feeling well.

Apparently, by the time the paramedic came, Hemapala had stopped breathing. He was given artificial respiration, but to no effect.

The LTTE removed Hemapala's body to another place, taking two men to keep vigil by it. The next day undertakers came and took the body away. They embalmed it in some way and brought it in a coffin back to the camp. We all filed past it to pay our last respects to Hemapala. Then I was sent to hand the body over to the ICRC. I asked if I could take Ratnapala with me, as Ratnapala had been the dead man's closest associate. We took the coffin to the LTTE's political headquarters at Kilinochchi where it was given a quick gun salute. When we handed it over to the ICRC, I gave testimony that it had been a natural death. The body would then have been returned to Hemapala's family, in Anuradhapura.

Hemapala had grown tired of life. But his death was a shock to us all and a blow to everyone's morale. For a week or two everyone was quiet and there was no laughter. Even those who hadn't liked Hemapala were very sad. We felt that if he had lived he would have been the first to be sent home—being the eldest of us and a civilian.

29

Frustration was mounting. We had been back under Sangeethan's rule for a few months and in captivity for nearly six years. There was still no sign of the Government. Nothing had come of any application we made directly to the LTTE either. With Sangeethan in charge, there were measures in place to make sure no one—neither us nor our guards—could relax.

Another Cricket World Cup had come and gone: this time the Sri Lankan team had been badly routed. The LTTE had just carried out a suicide attack on the President at an election rally. She survived, but lost an eye. We were entering a new millennium and still the war staggered on.

The boys grew disgruntled. One day, some of them refused the lunch that was brought. They said they didn't like the food. Sangeethan sent someone to ask why they weren't eating. Amerasinghe started an argument with the guy who came. Sangeethan ordered Amerasinghe out of the cell. We didn't know where they'd taken him. I suggested we should all refuse food until Amerasinghe was brought back. After a night he came back. He had been locked in a dog cage as punishment for his outburst. After that, I reminded the boys they should let me handle disputes.

Then one day the guards came and selected three guys—Amerasinghe; Jayantha Bandara and Kumara. These three were the eldest of the Army prisoners. The guards came in and told them to collect their belongings. We assumed they were moving them to another cell. Later we learnt that they had been released. The LTTE's chief political strategist was sick. The LTTE wanted the Government to airlift him to medical care. They released three prisoners in return for the favour. The Tigers couldn't take the risk of fully breaking with the state, you see. Eelam was not an actual state and there were times when the LTTE themselves needed the help of a government.

The guards said nothing to us. I imagine they did not want to provoke any feeling in the remaining prisoners. Later we asked where our comrades had been taken. That's when they told us they had been released. It gave us some hope. Perhaps it also made some of us restless and impatient for a change in our own circumstances.

* * *

The talk of a hunger strike began in the other cell. That was the cell in which most of the younger soldiers were held. I was in one with a slightly older, more sober crowd. So we didn't learn about this idea until it was brought up at our next ICRC visit. The ICRC delegate was a little alarmed. He advised against it. He said we weren't strong enough to go on a hunger strike. They interviewed us one by one to ask about the idea. To discuss the hunger strike with the whole group would have made the ICRC party to the action.

When they came to me I said I was not for it. For the LTTE to take any notice of it—for it to change anything—it would have to be a strike against the Government. If I went on hunger strike and died in the effort, the Navy could choose to call it suicide or treachery. My family might lose all benefits from the Navy. I did not want to risk this. I said I didn't want to be a part of it. Vijitha followed my lead. Most of the others decided they would go on strike.

The ICRC had discussed our idea with the LTTE too, since the Army boys were adamant. I imagine the LTTE loved the idea. It could only give them political mileage. After a period of no communication with the Government, this might also offer some way to re-start any negotiations. They would not have to start the conversation—the prisoners' strike would do it.

The boys set a date to start their strike. The ICRC made sure we had another emergency meeting just before that date. This time they came with a doctor who conducted an examination on each of us. Again, they asked us individually if we wanted to go on this strike. They wanted to make sure those joining were doing it of their own volition—that we had not been forced into it by the LTTE. They maintained that they wished to discourage us. They were the only concerned party at hand. By this point nobody was interested in us but the ICRC and our families. And we couldn't talk to our families.

On the morning of the day appointed for the strike to begin, everyone in the other cell refused their meals. The guards came to our cell next. I said I would take my meals, as did Vijitha and one other guy. We went on like this for three days. The boys on hunger strike were accepting water but nothing else.

The LTTE showed no sign of concern. At this point, I began to feel that I had been wrong not to join the others. I, twenty years older than many of these boys, played the role of a surrogate father and leader to them. I should not be standing apart from their struggle. I also wondered if it would raise the profile of the strike if I joined it.

I asked the men in my cell if they were committed to seeing it through. They said they were. Vijitha and the other soldier who had abstained also said they were ready to join. From the third day, we all went on strike.

30

It gave everyone a boost that we were now all in. I think it was on about the fifth day that the LTTE decided it was time to take our strike to the media. They took off our chains and drove us into the town. They had arranged mats and pillows and blankets for us at a school in Puthukkudiyiruppu town. We were taken there and laid out on show. These were the first pillows and blankets we'd seen in captivity, of course. The LTTE went to town. They allowed the public to file past us. They invited the media in: selected international media and the Jaffna correspondents of local media outlets.

After the seventh day the LTTE delivered their master stroke. They said they welcomed our families. If they wished to come and visit us, they would be allowed into LTTE controlled territory. They said they would accommodate and provide for our families— this message should be conveyed to them through the ICRC.

What they knew of course was that our families would still need Government approval to cross into the North, at Omanthai. The President did not respond. The LTTE looked set to win the round.

By this point Somapala had got so weak he had to be taken to hospital and given saline. The strike had been going on for nine days. There was an ICRC doctor monitoring our blood pressure, as well as an LTTE doctor attending us. We were beginning to lose mental focus.

I had to take some action. That night, while there were no visitors around, I told the others that from the tenth day I alone would stop accepting water. I told the LTTE cadre in charge. Of course the decision was reported in the media, along with an account of my deteriorating condition.

At this point, the President agreed that two people from each prisoner's family could be given clearance to travel north to us. The news was communicated to us by both the LTTE and the ICRC. This would have been about midday on the eleventh day. I can't now imagine how we ever took in such news. I told Vijitha and the others not to get too excited beforehand. I was afraid our weakened bodies could not handle excitement. The authorities asked me to start drinking water again, which I did.

The next day our families set off from home. In those times it wasn't a journey you could do easily in a day. The roads were bad; there were many checkpoints and you certainly would not travel after dark. So our families spent the night at a Navy camp in Medavachchiya. There is a story about this stop I only just learnt, when I met the man who had then been commander of this camp and province. He told me that the Navy had arranged more comfortable accommodation for my wife on account of her being the wife of a ranking officer. But Chandani had politely declined it. She said she would also go into the communal sleeping area that had been arranged for the other families. She said she would stand with the other families just as her husband stood with the other prisoners.

On the twelfth day our families were brought in and a terrible drama began to unfold. There must have been close to thirty people in the party. They came in all at once, accompanied by many LTTE people, everyone looking anxiously for their own amongst the prisoners. From our sleeping mats we looked back, trying to spot faces we knew in the crowd.

I caught sight of my wife almost straight away and looked for my children. When I saw my older brother too, I realised my sons were not in the party. I didn't ask why at that point. We were really in no state for anything as emotionally overwhelming as that moment. Everyone was crying; there were no smiles. My wife was scared to hold me. I'd got so like a skeleton she was afraid of breaking my bones.

After a while, the commotion subsided and then each family sat anxiously by their own prisoner, oblivious to the rest of the room. My wife explained why she hadn't brought the children. With only two people from each family allowed, she had wisely decided it would be unfair to choose between the boys. So she brought my brother with her instead. I had not had the where-withal to think this through and was disappointed not to see the children.

By the next day, we had all recovered a little and the parents of the prisoners started making requests to the LTTE to release us. Thamilchelvan[35] agreed to meet with them, representing the political leadership. He said of course the LTTE was prepared to release their sons but a Government representative would be needed to negotiate this. So, the LTTE's strategic use of the hunger strike continued. In the South, politicians scrambled to make their own mileage out of the event. MPs spoke to the media, volunteering themselves as brokers.

Of course it was not to be. So, the LTTE told the families to go home and lobby their own government. They told the parents of the prisoners they should ask their sons to suspend their hunger strike until a negotiation could be set up. Remember, most of the prisoners were boys when they were captured. Apart from my wife and Vijitha's wife, most of the family visitors were the parents of the prisoners.

These parents returned from the meeting and pleaded with their sons to give up the strike. They turned to me and asked me to tell their sons to stop. We all agreed we would suspend the strike. But we said if no change came, we would begin another strike unto death.

A grand lunch was arranged by the LTTE to mark the end of the hunger strike. It was really an opportunity for our families to eat well. They had not really felt like eating much while we starved ourselves. The prisoners were not strong enough to join. We drank milk and ate fruit. The families were accommodated for another two days so that they could see us grow a little stronger.

Once we were in a better state, we met each other's families. I also explained to my fellow prisoners why I had not originally joined the strike. But I said I was happy now that I had. We had been able to see our families, even if we had not been released.

The LTTE had not been idle during the strike. I saw intelligence staff chatting to people from the South and hoped the ICRC had briefed our families on this sort of thing. Vijitha's wife handed over a letter, written by his now nearly seven year old daughter to the LTTE Leader, Prabhakaran, asking for Vijitha's release.

Meanwhile another offer was made to me. Sangeethan came to see me and said again that my release could be arranged if I agreed to work covertly for the LTTE. He said I could take anyone with me that I wanted to take. I told my wife this proposition had been made. I said I would prefer to stay in captivity than to have my children grow up the sons of a traitor. But I told her she could make the decision. Without hesitation, she said she would support me in my choice. Sangeethan had already approached her and asked her to persuade me to accept their offer.

After two days the families were ready to leave. Everyone wondered if some prisoners might be allowed to go with them—and whom. Indeed, three of our number were released. The LTTE called it a gift to the parents. These were Somapala, Vijitha and Anura. For the rest of us, it was not an easy thing to part with our families.

For the first time, I felt glad that my children had not come and would not have to go through this second separation. I learnt later that they had of course been terrified even at the prospect that their mother would travel to the North. What if they ended up losing both their parents?

Thinking back on the hunger strike now I remember that the government had already begun to suspect me of treachery before any of this happened. It makes a slight mockery of my feeling that we should not take an action that could be construed as being against the state. But in this I had been right: everything that happened, happened because the LTTE wanted it.

It was a circus. We went from being prisoners to being exhibits for the media. When I opted to stop drinking water it was a gesture of urgency rather than deep thought. I was already losing focus, from hunger and weakness. But I also felt a desperation in the boys that nothing was happening. I had to find a way of raising the stakes. It was not unlike the instinctive reactions you feel on the battlefront.

It was not easy returning to the camp. There were some changes though. The parents had made a plea to the LTTE to have our chains removed. On our return to the camp we were not put back in chains. After a little practice we learnt to walk again. Most of all, it released our minds a little. With Vijitha gone home, one of my key responsibilities had also been lifted from my shoulders. And within a few weeks, Sangeethan left and Newton came back.

PART III

31

A new cell block was built for us, with more light and air than we'd had before. We were put in one room, all together. It was a large hall, twenty feet long, with a half-wall going round it. From the top of the half-wall to the ceiling was a concertina grate that could be pulled back during the day.

We could not have guessed we would see this sort of change. The hunger strike had escalated to a significance we never imagined when we started it. You asked me whether I considered the risks of going on the strike and seeing it through. Sitting here now, I can see what you mean. I am free and well and level-headed: I have all those things to lose. At that time I inhabited a very different reality. We were eighteen forgotten men. We believed our government had given us up for dead. Six years is a long time to carry on neither living nor dying. The hunger strike may look like a political strategy now but we were not in charge of it. In truth it was a foolish act of desperation that turned out very well.

We spent our days outside now. Our cell was opened up in the morning and we were only locked into it again at bedtime. We could shower in the evening and eat dinner outdoors before we had to go back into our cell together. Eventually, they even gave us the key so that we could let ourselves out in the morning and lock our own cell at night.

We never strayed far, though. A new space had been cleared in the jungle for our living quarters and we kept to its lines. If we were going to walk more than a few steps we would call out to the guard to let him know. If we had to call for a paramedic in the night we would do it from inside our locked cell.

For the first time, we had a stillness of mind. Living in the jungle was already a respite. We were surrounded by tall mahogany trees that must have grown there for two hundred years. It was a shaded area, with less undergrowth. There was just a dark, fertile, soil underfoot. It could still be hot, during the day. Even the winds that blew through were hot, dry winds. But we didn't mind so much, outdoors. We could drag our sleeping mats out and spend our days under the trees.

By now we only really spoke to each other if something new happened or, in the case of some of the younger men, to bicker about small things. There was less squabbling than there been before. It only started up again when the rains came and we had to stay indoors. Even then, there were games of noughts and crosses played on the floor. The ICRC had supplied us with playing cards too. We were also all readers. There were a lot of Sinhala novels sent to us that we would read and pass from prisoner to prisoner.

We were gradually regaining at least a mental privacy. With my ship-mate Vijitha released, I no longer had to worry about buoying up his spirits. After breakfast I would pick up a book. If I read lying down I would drift in and out of sleep until the longest part of the day was over. We always had weekend papers to read from a few months before, stockpiled by the ICRC before each of their meetings with us. I would read in the papers about new books and then ask for those to be brought the next time. I even read a number of books about the Tigers, which I'm surprised they allowed.

Our room felt more like a dormitory than a cell now. I think we adjusted quickly to a more peaceful state of mind and avoided looking back at darker times. A bid to starve ourselves had in fact resulted in our becoming human again. We'd had our first exposure to the world at large. We'd seen our families. We had begun to believe that a release might come. Perhaps this event had made us come alive to our captors too. When, after the hunger strike, the parents of the younger soldiers went to the Tiger administration with their smaller appeals, each one was granted. We would not be chained again. We would be allowed to receive parcels from home.

We had some contact with outsiders too, as a few selected media personnel were allowed to come in now and interview us. Contact of this kind also gave us a sense of connection to the world outside. We were no longer completely concealed from the world. Journalists had started to visit my family in Colombo too, to hear about their experience since my capture. You have to realise that this was the first time—six years into my captivity—that the world at large had seemed interested at all.

Our kitchen facilities were restored and on our return to the camp we began to live very well. Our ICRC deliveries had grown to luxurious proportions, with the ICRC providing everything we thought to ask for. We now received the original milk powder, sugar, chilli powder and dhal as well as cooking oil, noodles, spices, curry powders, other lentils, canned fish, tea, coffee, fruit cordials, soap, toothbrushes, toothpaste and cigarettes.

On top of all this, we began to receive parcels from home. It had been agreed the parcels should not be more than one cubic foot in size and would be examined by both the ICRC and the LTTE for glass containers and other suspicious materials. The inspection was carried out with ever decreasing vigilance. We shared the food that we received from home and kept personal items for ourselves. Sometimes now our cell would smell like a heady competition of colognes.

We suspected that some families were running through the salaries of their captured sons, leaving nothing for their return. So, we were careful what we asked for. More expensive requests were reserved for my more affluent family. From them we received stock cubes, dried leaf congee, marmite and a favoured Chinese chilli paste that we could use to make our soups taste better. My wife would also send me books to supplement the ICRC stock and my mother in law would slip in religious texts. Others received home-made sweets and pickles.

Between the ICRC and our families we had better treats than our captors. Every time we received a parcel or cooked something special, we would send a little to the guards. We were happier to do this, now we had been placed under Newton's care again. This event was welcomed by all the prisoners. Newton was everyone's favourite jailer.

32

I don't believe that Newton, or indeed the rest of the LTTE, bore us any specific animosity. We were the enemy only according to our institution. Newton always maintained that he hoped we would get to go home. He felt it would be possible. He remained optimistic about the future, unlike many other cadres I had met.

This gentle, soft-spoken man, doing his best to reassure his prisoners, was reputedly one of the best and most ruthless bomb experts the LTTE had. I never saw him get angry. He must have been about ten years younger than I was. He always addressed me respectfully as 'sir', according to my naval rank.

He talked a lot about his brother, who worked at Puthukku-diyiruppu hospital. I can't help thinking that the family men amongst the cadres lost their battlefront mentality in favour of something more subtle. The simple fact they got to go home at night must have made a difference. Newton himself was from Batticaloa. He was married to a woman from Jaffna who taught at the secondary school in Puthukkudiyiruppu. They had two young daughters at the time.

I knew Newton trusted me when he began placing his daughters in my care. On days when he brought them to work with him, Newton would send the girls over to our block. They addressed us all as 'uncle' and enjoyed the cream biscuits from our ICRC rations. Newton used to joke that his daughters were most interested in the enemy and never wanted to spend time anywhere else in the camp. We'd talk to them and sometimes feed them whatever we had cooked for lunch.

The girls must have been about three and six. The older one certainly knew we were prisoners and something about the conflict. I told her to bring her sister and her parents and come and visit my own children in the South, after peace had dawned. 'Our Appa can't leave the Vanni,' she said. 'He will be arrested'.

One day, Newton came and asked us if there were any of us who played badminton. It turned out he was a keen player and had no one to play against. At his suggestion, we created a court outside our cell and at the next ICRC visit we asked if they would provide us with nets, racquets, and shuttlecocks. The ICRC jumped at the idea. Ever after, two or three new canisters of shuttlecocks would arrive with every ICRC delegation.

It was perhaps an odd time to be playing friendly games of badminton, while the political pendulum was swinging wildly. On the battlefield, each side bungled successive operations. The LTTE had sustained major losses and was marooned in the Vanni for a time. Still, at four o'clock in the evening, LTTE cadres would come to lead us to our court.

Occasionally visiting teams would come to play us at badminton or at cricket. These had to be people the Tigers trusted. We had tournament days. We were told the night before that there was to be a tournament. It was our job to get together biscuits, fruit cordials and milk tea for the breaks. With our ICRC treats the prisoners were best placed to play host to the visitors. We had by now also built a summer house near our cell and kitchen and badminton court.

But on tournament days, we would be led from our own area to the full grounds cleared elsewhere in the jungle for the LTTE's training exercises. A pitch had been laid for cricket. The prisoners were stronger cricketers. I think we had grown up playing more of it, in schools in the South. Newton would always work himself into the winning side. We, as a matter of deference, would make him captain.

Now we had tracksuit bottoms sent to us by our families and tennis shoes sent by the ICRC. So, we didn't really look that different to our opponents on the field. Some of the other LTTE cadres, not just Newton, would join the prisoners' team. Plus when it came to cricket we all supported the national team. Our spirits were good.

Often, after the games, Newton and I would sit in the summer house and chat. The others hung around, but really it was he and I who talked. We talked about important things, but not in a systematic way. We shared details of our families and drifted into politics. Our views were not so different from each other, if you think about it. Newton's experience as a Tamil man in Sri Lanka, especially over the riot years, had made him believe that there was need for an autonomous Tamil homeland. My experience of the war had made me believe some form of regional devolution was due.

You asked me if I also had political conversations with my fellow prisoners. I have to admit that I avoided it. Think about the way parents are always disappointed when their children choose guns out of all the toys available. Just as young LTTE cadres could be more absolute about fighting the enemy, so it was the same with young soldiers in the Government forces. In the early days my fellow prisoners had shown a lot of anger towards the LTTE for keeping them captive. Gradually they had relaxed. I didn't want political discussion to re-awaken the old animosity. I felt it was my job to keep them calm.

I don't blame them. They were prisoners bridling against their jailers. They were also young boys who had given their lives to fighting a war, perhaps without the political exposure really to have thought about it. This was another way in which I felt my captivity to be a more solitary than communal experience.

In any case, a radio had now come into our lives, renewing our daily connection to the world outside. Initially the ICRC sent us just one radio and soon arguments began about choosing a frequency. So, after the hunger strike, people started to ask their families to send them transistor radios in their next parcel. For me the radio brought a chance to listen to new music again. I started writing down the lyrics of songs I liked. I'd scribble them down as best I could while listening to the song. Then I'd fill in the gaps when I heard it again. Gradually the other prisoners started to call out to me, asking me to add their favourites to the notebooks I was keeping. I filled two big notebooks with song lyrics. After my release, people out in the world were confused how I knew the words to songs that had been released while I was in the jungle.

During my captivity I filled many notebooks, in fact. Some of these I still have with me today. To pass the time I would copy out interesting or informative articles—about history, about health matters, about show business. I took down notes on grammar and lists of book titles. I cut out articles from the English and Sinhala papers and pasted them into my notebooks. The ICRC actually gave us appointments diaries and I kept brief journals in those. Only one of them survived. Over the years there were moments when we were made to destroy the things we had collected. This was usually when we had to move in a rush, or when the guards were angry.

But in these better days, it wasn't only music we heard. Our radios eventually brought news of elections and a coming transfer of power. We didn't live in hope but we had a sense that change may be at hand. At least it was possible. We did not think our release imminent. I knew, and Newton agreed, there was a serious deadlock that a new government would have first to break. But we were beginning to hear hopeful stories filtering up from the South. I can't say that there wasn't a slight change in our moods.

33

Life was very different now. We locked our own cell at night and it was only to go to the well we had to ask permission, since other people also used it and we were not allowed to meet them. We had our own place in the jungle. We really did not feel this period to be one of hardship. But we would still be here some time. Two years passed after the hunger strike before we began to see any prospect of going home.

First, a few more of our number were released—after a visit of the Association of Parents of Missing Soldiers. Now we were down to the last seven of our original twenty-two. But we weren't counting the days. We had learnt that we could not live in a state of anticipation. And we knew of obstacles in our way. The President had made it very clear she was not prepared to negotiate unless the LTTE laid down their arms. Everyone knew they would not. There would need to be a new government even to break the impasse.

Newton agreed with me that nothing dramatic could be expected. Yet I felt I was now constantly listening out for a change. Newton told me some efforts were being made. I trusted this information, coming from him. But I kept it to myself, rather than get everyone's hopes up.

After the elections in December 2001, we had a period of national—or perhaps divided—government. We had an incumbent President of one party and a new Parliament led by the opposing party. The incoming party had promised new negotiations in their election manifesto. There were two aspects of these talks that affected us directly. One was obviously the negotiation for the release of prisoners. The other was negotiation for prisoners' access to their families, on both sides. In this context, the ICRC made a request to the Government and the LTTE, to allow us a visit from our families. It was agreed. I think ICRC intended the visit as a kind of preliminary reunion. This way we and our families would have a preparatory sense of each other, so we knew how to prepare for the final release.

The ICRC told us, at one of our regular meetings, that there was a possibility of a family visit. The next we heard of it was the day before the visit happened. We were told to pack some things—I don't remember that we were told why. We knew it was something special—we never had to pack for a regular ICRC meeting and by this point we knew we were not moving camps.

We were brought to a renovated holiday bungalow near Mallawi. It was a nice house with every amenity, purpose built for state guests. These were the sorts of properties the LTTE prepared for guests, especially at times of negotiation like this one. They never held back when they had a point to prove. We were not accustomed to things like beds.

The ICRC brought our families to the place. This was May 2002, more than two years since I'd last seen my wife at the hunger strike. I was seeing my children after nearly eight years. My wife had sent me photographs of the boys through the ICRC, but I was still taken aback by how big and tall they were and how much I didn't know them. I would not have recognised my youngest son at all, if it hadn't been for the pictures. He was only two when I was captured; now he was ten and about to form his first conscious memory of his father. He knew me only from a framed photograph my wife kept in the house. Sometimes she would buy him gifts and tell him they were from his father. She'd written to me that one birthday he placed my photograph on the floor so that he could show me what he was doing with the new toy car he thought I'd sent him.

My youngest boy thought all men were uncles. Indeed my boys were greatly indebted to uncles and aunts. My friends, batchmates and relatives had made great efforts to give them fatherly support while I was absent. My closest friend, Tissera Samarasinghe, called my wife and sons each evening before he went home from work. He did this every day without fail, for entire duration of my captivity. My sister never took her own children on holiday without asking my boys to join them. So many others also tried in whatever way they could, to see that my family felt cared for in my absence.

Apparently on the journey north my elder boys Shamal and Manil teased the youngest, Lahiru, that he had better not mistake his Appachchi for another uncle. So the little one chanted 'Appachchi, Appachchi,' all the way, to fix the word in his mind. He was now older than his elder brothers had been when I was captured. He was naturally a little shy with me at first, but gradually came to know me as his father. My older boys were 15 and 17; the eldest had just completed his O-levels. I had already missed their growing up. There are some things irredeemably lost in any captivity, and mine was to lose those years with my children. I could be reunited with them but I could not go back and live alongside them through their childhoods, seeing them change. I couldn't recover the years I had missed or what would have grown between us if we'd had them.

Yet suddenly we were holidaying together. We were just in this place to relax and spend time with our families. The LTTE did all the work. When the LTTE wanted to give you a treat, they really treated you. We had every kind of food we could imagine—tables heaped with jumbo prawns and the finest catch of crab. Someone's uncle had brought a bottle of arrack with him. It was my first drink since I was captured.

They took our families on outings, each with a clear intention. There were trips to see LTTE graveyards, or sleeping houses as they were called. The word was that these fallen cadres would rise to see the liberation of their people at the dawn of Eelam. That was how they motivated children to fight. All the graves were named and numbered. We were taken to Mullaitivu shores—to show us how the LTTE had wrestled this territory from the government. We saw the wreck of a ship they had captured.

But this visit included no petitions or meetings with high ranking LTTE officials. It was just a visit for the families. Again, it was mostly a visit of parents to their sons. I was the only married prisoner remaining—Vijitha, Amerasinghe and Nomis had been released. I was also the only prisoner with children. There was no tight restriction on number this time and special care had been taken that my wife should be able to bring our boys to see me. Sometimes the other families took our children out, so my wife and I could have the time alone we had also not had in years.

My children had never seen the North. For them it was an exposure to the world of Eelam: to a gun culture and to the destruction that war had wreaked on this place and the people in it. I suppose it was quite educational.

When everyone left, it was with some optimism that the war would end. More particularly, we and our families were confident that our captivity would end. This was a lighter goodbye than the one we'd had to go through after the hunger strike. Now we believed that it wouldn't be long till we saw our families again, as free men. We went back to our life in the camp and waited for good news.

* * *

Then one day, at the end of August, Newton came and told us it had been arranged. We would be going home. We were told to pack our things and wait for a bus that would take us to Kilinochchi the next day. From there we would be released, he said.

Can you imagine?

We didn't hesitate. We quickly packed our personal things and I the library of books I had collected. Everything else, we gave away. All our ICRC stocks went to the cadres—biscuits, milk powder, new t-shirts. Overjoyed and overexcited we never stopped for pause, as if the decision might change if we didn't seize it fast. By early morning we were ready for the bus.

Did we experience vertigo? No, not yet. The joy of going home didn't leave any room for doubt. Also, we would not know until we actually went home how much we had become prisoners; how much of this way of life was now inside us.

Lunchtime came. There was no sign of the bus. They had to send us lunch from the LTTE kitchens, since we no longer had our cooking stocks. Some of our guards came and had lunch with us. They kept reassuring us that the bus was on its way. But we were worried.

Our anxiety progressed into the evening. Then we were told that there had been some legal problem. Our release had been postponed.

It came like a falling sky. Almost everyone was in tears—the disappointment was too great. We worried that the negotiations had met with some insurmountable political obstacle. We were restless and fretful. We had already lost our facility in coping with suspense. Suddenly it mattered again to us that we had no information, no prospects, no dates, nothing to look forward to.

34

Newton came to tell us what had happened. Although an agreement had been reached, at the last moment the Government and the Supreme Court refused to authorise the release of Kennedy, the prisoner the LTTE most wanted back. Kennedy was being swapped for me—ours was the only direct exchange. So the overall agreement was held up.

Initially the mood was one of disgust. The boys were frustrated and angry. I felt I had to talk them back into life in the camp. I tried to reason with them that at least now we knew release would come, even if we did not know when. I said let's wait, let's not do anything rash now that could ruin it. It could be a month, it could be six; it would be nothing to the long years of uncertainty we had already endured. I felt it was my job to cool their young blood.

The next few weeks were a little different: we were waiting for a change. At our evening games Newton would reassure us. He said there were hurdles but things were moving and we would get past them. What we heard on the radio seemed to corroborate his story. The time we spent waiting felt long but it was less than a month, in reality.

Then it was confirmed again. A date was given—for a week later. Then it was postponed by a few days. But finally Newton came to assure us the bus was really on its way. We would be leaving the next day. He was confident this was the moment, so I was confident too.

Newton was there to put us on the bus himself. He'd brought his daughters with him again to say goodbye to us. Subha and Darshi gave each of the prisoners a framed photograph of them-selves—taken in a studio—to carry away as a keepsake. I have mine to this day.

It was a heart-breaking departure, if you can believe that. We had been living with all of these cadres for so long that there was a kind of brotherly understanding between us. We were taking leave of a family we would probably never see again.

Newton was in tears and for me it was hardest saying goodbye to him. Between us there had never been any antagonism. Even at the start, Newton and I had never felt like enemies or oppo-nents or men of different races. Our interaction was always cor-dial and increasingly full of friendship. Newton had only ever tried to help us. He had always treated his prisoners as his equals. We were all sorry to say goodbye to him.

I said to Newton 'who knows, we may meet again—either in your vision of Eelam or in my vision of a united federal state'. He smiled in return, but didn't make any repartee. I think about this now. At that moment, he could not have expected what was coming for them. It was an optimistic time: we thought perhaps an end was near, and without further bloodshed. I think the LTTE believed they might get reasonable autonomy out of this round of talks. I think they might have accepted a settlement. Unfortunately the new Government in the South also lacked leaders with the will and the courage to put the settlement above their own immediate political gains. We were all to pay heavily for the loss of this moment. The longer the war went on, the less likely it was to end without extreme brutality.

I think this was also why the cadres we had known were sad to see us go. I don't mean Newton, in this instance, but the younger guys. It must have been hard to watch us being freed while they remained, essentially, in captivity. I remembered the story of Mohan's mother, who said to him 'you have lost your own freedom by seeking it for others.' A lot of these cadres, even the ones who joined the LTTE voluntarily, joined as teenagers. That is when the mind is more open to militancy. But eventually you want more of life than a singular cause.

This is why I believe that thirty years of fighting wouldn't do. If the LTTE wanted to achieve any of its goals it needed to achieve them in ten years. It isn't only the cadres who became frustrated. You think how difficult it is for an elected government to keep popular support for more than a decade. How much less likely is it then that a self-appointed militia would keep the support of its people? There's a limit to anyone's tolerance of anything.

But here we were, seven prisoners leaving for better lives than our captors could hope for. The bus came. We got in, waved good-bye, and started the journey back.

35

My emotions were mixed, driving out of the camp. Eight years is a long time. I had become unconsciously attuned to the environment I inhabited. I was now leaving for another country and felt the weight of passage. But any sense of loss was greatly outweighed by my joy. I was going to be released. I was going home. I didn't know what those things meant, exactly, but I was very happy about them. We were, all seven of us, in a very cheerful mood.

There was a world to look at outside the window. What did we know? We knew we were being released. We knew it would be an exchange of prisoners. I knew that I was being exchanged for Kennedy. But I suppose we did not know exactly how the exchange would take place.

We were to spend the night in Kilinochchi before being driven to Omanthai the next morning, which during the war marked the border on the main road between North and South. The exchange would take place in the No Man's Land between Government and LTTE territory. In Kilinochchi we were met by the LTTE's Media Spokesman. He hosted us to a good thosai dinner at one of their new cafeterias on the main A9 road. They wished us all the best for the future. You see, when the LTTE wished to act like a government, it did so in style. There were photographs taken, which I knew would later be used for the purposes of their propaganda and fundraising. There had been no other prisoner exchange between the Government and the LTTE. Both sides wanted to give it a ceremonial feeling.

We were put up for the night at a sort of LTTE hotel, over-looking Iranamadu tank. We slept in beds. A tailor came to take our measurements. By morning there were new 'release-suits' for all of us—black trousers with a white shirt. We got up and got dressed and the LTTE took us to the ICRC delegation office in Kilinochchi. There was still some time before we had to set off to make the appointed hour for the exchange. We had tea at the ICRC office. When we finally left, we did so in an ICRC bus. I think according to protocol we could not enter the No Man's Land in an LTTE vehicle. But they provided us motorcycle out-riders! The riders were LTTE police in ceremonial uniforms, riding in an arrow formation. It felt like a state drive.

By now I had started to feel a little nervous. My mind was not very clear. Were we free yet? Or were we still prisoners? I felt that my body did not know how to move freely, receiving these mixed signals from my mind.

Driving up to the point of exchange, we saw there were already crowds there, awaiting our arrival. They had put up stages with decorated canopies. It was an overwhelming prospect. We were marched in, as though entering an arena. There were front row seats reserved for us from which we could look across to our families on the other side. My wife was there with my mother. My two brothers and their wives were also there. They were all here to take me home but we had to remain separate until the official exchange had taken place. We smiled and waved.

Looking across at my family I felt again the thing I had sus-pected—that my father had died while I was in captivity. At some point his letters had stopped. The rest of my family also stopped mentioning him in their letters to me. I guessed what had happened but I never had the courage to ask, outright.

There were many officials in attendance today. The Government's representatives included the Navy Commander and the Army Commander, along with other senior officers. The Defence Secretary was also present. I immediately noticed Selvaratnam among the LTTE representatives, along with the LTTE's military commander and the head of the LTTE artillery wing. I think Karuna may also have been there. I think he was still a part of the LTTE at this time. I can't remember if Soosai was there. Suda Master, Daya Master and Uncle George the translator were all there too. It was an incredible and hopeful gesture: this gathering of important people from both sides of the conflict. There were also many media representatives.

The ceremony started and speeches were made. The Army Commander spoke; then the Defence Secretary. They said they welcomed the prisoner exchange and made assurances that it marked the beginning of a new era. There was talk of a long war past and a long awaited peace to come. I can't remember who it was who spoke from the LTTE—but one of the high ups. The exchange was made into a great symbolic occasion.

After the ceremony the prisoners were lined up and we walked toward each other, shaking hands as we crossed sides. The LTTE prisoners were dressed exactly as we were. We were sportsmen after a match.

There were thirteen LTTE cadres being swapped for the seven of us. Eleven prisoners were being released back to the LTTE. They had stated they wished to return to the movement. Two were released directly to their families because they had stated they wished to leave the movement. There had originally been three other prisoners also requested, but the LTTE had later removed their names from the list. They said there had been an error; those prisoners had been found not to be LTTE members. It is possible this amendment was made because the cadres in question were under 18. To acknowledge them as members of the movement would have been, accidentally, to concede that the LTTE did recruit child soldiers.

The Government had also withheld three other prisoners on the LTTE list. One of them was a cadre charged with involvement in the Town Hall bombing that took out the President's eye. The two others also had serious charges against them. The LTTE insisted that the seven prisoners they were releasing were the last they had in custody. That said, seven soldiers had just been captured by the LTTE in Trincomalee, days earlier, in retaliation for the arrest of two Tiger cadres. Apparently, at our release, the subsequent release of these other prisoners was discussed by the two parties!

The only direct swap was my release in exchange for the release of the Black Tiger, Kennedy. Jesumy Fernando, alias Kennedy, had led a group of nine cadres in infiltrating the Palaly air base in August 1994. They had attacked Air Force helicopters. Some cadres had been killed in the ensuing battle and Kennedy had been captured. The Attorney General had agreed to lift the indictments against him so he could be released today, with the Air Force Commander agreeing that he had no objections. We had spent similar periods in captivity; Kennedy had been captured about six weeks before I was.

Now the ceremony was over and we were free to join our families. The press surrounded us immediately, taking photographs of us meeting our families. You look surprised. Yes, it was a little overwhelming. Years later I saw a picture from that morning, in an exhibition in the National Gallery in Colombo. I was with my wife at the Gallery and a journalist must have captured us then too. The next day we saw in the newspapers a photograph of ourselves looking at a photograph of ourselves. On the day of our release what I said to the press was that no one on either side should find themselves again in the position we had been in. That was really my wish: that this should be a moment of change.

Others also came and spoke to our families. Selvaratnam and Suda Master came to meet mine. I heard later that one of my seniors from the Navy had a long conversation with Selvaratnam. When he reported it to me I smiled because Selvaratnam's views had not changed in the eight years since he and I had talked. I spoke to him too as we shook hands to say goodbye. He had made a point of coming over to speak to me though we had not seen each other since I was handed out of his custody seven years before. I reminded him that the LTTE had not achieved an independent state of Eelam by the year 2000, as he had sworn they would. I told him that I still had respect for their cause but the same reservations about their means. It was a friendly exchange. Now, I think again what a missed opportunity it was to have failed at the peace talks of 1994. That was a moment to have achieved something. But neither side had the political maturity to do it.

Even beyond my own family, I was today meeting a lot of people after a long time. The now Navy Commander had been my Sailing Authority when I took my last voyage on the *Sagarawardene*. It was good to see him.

I also spoke to Kennedy—tied as our fates had been to each other. We didn't know each other, we just said hello. Later, I read newspaper reports of him with interest and asked questions about what had become of him. I know he was taken back into the organisation—I don't know if he had also to face charges for letting himself fall into enemy hands without swallowing cyanide.[36] He was a Black Tiger after all and weakness was not tolerated. I can only imagine that either he got away from the

LTTE at some point or he stayed and was killed in the final battles.

This time when we clambered into buses, they were Army vehicles. We boarded them with our families. We were apparently now free: military men on our way to lunch at brigade head-quarters in Vavuniya. I think the ceremony had begun at an auspicious time around 10 o'clock—by about 11.30 we were on our way.

The LTTE travelled in the opposite direction, with their people. All ICRC responsibilities ceased. This was when we really moved worlds. When our lunch was served, it tasted like the sort of food we used to eat at home in the South. At one point the Navy Commander, mistaking my older brother for me, said to him 'Boya, eating well after a long time!' My brother had to say 'I'm not Ajith, I'm Lalith'. We looked alike and this often happened. There was no one from the press here; just the seven prisoners and their families and other people from the services.

The day of release had a note of sadness in it for me. My father could not be there to see it, despite all his efforts to secure it. He had made so many appeals on my behalf, growing increas-ingly frustrated with leaders he had supported all his life. I now knew he had died over a year before, just a few days short of his seventy-eighth birthday.

From the brigade headquarters at Vavuniya we were flown directly to Colombo in an M-16 troop carrier. We landed on the Army grounds at Galle Face—here my children were waiting for me, with my brother-in-law and one of my batchmates. We were driven to Temple Trees to meet the Prime Minister; previously the Leader of the Opposition to whom we'd written from captiv-ity. There was another tea laid on for us. I suppose it must have been about 3 or 4 o'clock.

The Prime Minister made a short casual address and expressed a wish to support us, on our return. I used that moment to make a representation I had promised to make on behalf of the last seven prisoners. While we were in captivity, one of them had said to me repeatedly that even if he got out he would have to live on the street. He said his family had spent all of his salary that they received while he was in captivity. There would be nothing for him when he returned. I promised him that if I was lucky enough to go home, I would make sure he had a roof over his head.

What I said to the Prime Minister was that these soldiers had joined the Forces as boys, spent months in training and had then been captured in active combat. Their adult lives to date had been given entirely in the service of their country. I said they were now of an age to marry but if they spent years working to save money to provide for families, they would be old men before they had the means to marry. I suggested that the country owed them a good start to their lives as free men. Perhaps they could be provided with housing? The Prime Minister asked his Media Coordinator to make a note of the request and mentioned that Dr Lalith Kotelawala of the Ceylinco Corporation was doing this sort of thing, privately.

After the tea at Temple Trees, the official ceremonies were truly over. We were free to leave as families. Our group of prisoners had already dispersed. We'd each of us spent the day with our own families and moved into separate worlds. We no longer belonged together. There were no big goodbyes.

* * *

This was my first time out on the roads of Colombo since 1994. It was now 2002.

We went, as a family, to observe rites at the Gangarama Temple. It was just a private visit we made and actually the only moment of quiet we had that day. When we got home, the house was already full of people. Everyone was there who had hoped and worked for my return. Everyone was also there who had never been to see my wife or children during my eight year captivity.

In those years there had been some people who were scared to associate themselves with the allegations against me. Oh yes, there had been a lot of that. Even my wife got worried about the stories and tried to find ways to stem them. She told one Tamil couple it might be better if they did not visit. This was a Mr and Mrs Kanagethram, from whom I had carried medicines to their relatives in Karainagar. Mr Kanagethram would not accept my wife's fears. But he asked his own wife to remove her pottu[37] when they came to visit my family. You know what it is to ask such a thing.

Now everyone was in my house to hear more stories, this time at least from me. I was tired and overwhelmed and wanted a night's sleep. There were even people from the press in my house. One journalist interviewed me for half an hour and drew the story out as a serial over several months.

HOMECOMING

36

I had missed a lot. I didn't know the neighbours. We had moved into a new house just before I was captured and I'd never had a chance to settle in. Our neighbours came to meet me for the first time. For the first week or so, the house was full of people. People came who knew us well; people came who didn't know us well. They asked the same questions, I gave the same answers. I did this again and again. I felt a little tired through that week.

There were things I had to do—I needed an ID card and a new driving licence. These things had got lost at sea on the night of my capture. I needed them to become a citizen again, with a bank account and all the other trappings. In my first week back, I met with an accident at Kohuwela roundabout. The collision wasn't my fault but I didn't have the wherewithal to avoid it. The ability to drive a car came back instinctively but the situation on the roads was new to me. It felt like there had been an explosion of cars in the city while I was away.

For the first months I was mostly preoccupied with finding ways to re-enter my family. You can't have these things back instantly. I had to wait for a way back into their lives. For the eight previous years my family had to be whole without me. There was no immediate role for me to play. I would say that I was more unfamiliar to them than familiar.

I realised that I could not tell my boys what to do and not to do; not when they had managed so many years without a father present. I realised that if I tried to force myself back into the lives of my wife and children I might release their anger at everything they'd had to live with for so long. It wasn't easy. Coming home was a reminder of what I had lost in captivity. My children were essentially grown up. I had missed their childhoods altogether. But the only thing I could do was to be patient. I had to allow time for a transition to occur naturally, rather than rush into the life I wanted back.

My own way of life had been entirely transformed while I was away. Above all I was not used to making any outward action on my own initiative. You have to realise that for eight years I'd done *everything* on instruction. Getting in and out of a jeep was determined by command. In captivity you're never the person who decides what you will do next. Re-learning autonomy was perhaps the hardest thing I had to do. In some ways it was harder to make this transition than it was to make the transition to being a prisoner. At least there you have no choice. There is just one way of doing things and someone else will tell you what that is. I found choice itself a difficult thing to get used to, once I returned.

When I wanted the toilet I looked around for someone whose permission to ask. I knew I was allowed to do these things by myself now but when I went to stand up I'd feel there was someone holding on to me, not letting me. The prison guard was inside me. I didn't want to talk about what I was going through. I felt no one else should know about the conversation I was having with myself. My aim was to make myself familiar to my family, not to explain to them how far away I was inside.

The world was different too. While I was away the country had moved into full-scale war and when I came back I felt that even civilians were battle hardened. People acted more mechanically. It was harder to locate a human touch. I felt that peaceful-ness had gone from the way we lived. Even the way people dressed seemed different, more ill at ease.

When I left, you hardly saw anyone in an office working at a computer. When I came back, everyone sat in front of a machine. Mobile phones weren't status symbols anymore—they were everywhere. The postman rarely came; the paper man had disap-peared altogether. You never stepped into a telephone box. It wasn't just the war of course. The reality I returned to was a more mercenary one. Compassion was not prized. Everyone was making money. I suppose I missed the decade in which all those changes had come of age. When I speak of the 70s and 80s now, they sound as exotic as the 30s and 40s.

I felt it even in the lives of my friends and relatives. Everyone now looked after his immediate family and avoided other people's concerns. And people had become afraid of speaking out. They were suspicious of each other.

When you're in the world you adjust to changes as they come. They become a part of you. But I felt I had dropped from the jungle into a new reality. I knew what had been in the letters of my closest family and friends and I knew what I had heard on the radio. But there was so much more that no one could have told me. My children were growing up in a world I did not know well enough for me to be any sort of guide to them.

I was worried that I would mess things up even if I tried just to help with their homework. I didn't know my children well enough to know how to suggest things to them. In the normal run of things, I would have known how to navigate their person-alities by this point in our lives. The boys admitted to their mother that I seemed more like an uncle, after all.

So, I went to watch them at rowing meets and I marked time. My elder boys were soon to leave school and become men on their own terms. With my youngest I could do a little more. I played badminton with him now and drove him to his sports practices.

But the world was still here. My wife had been mother and father both to our children. I don't think this was in any way easy with three young sons. She never collapsed. She found all the resources it took to weather those years alone. It gave me enormous courage in my own captivity to know that my wife was a woman of strong character. I knew she would keep our family going, out in the world. I knew that if I could just keep myself sane, I would come home to find she'd done the rest.

37

The Monday after I arrived home, I reported for duty. My signal had been released, giving my formal appointment as 'additional to Headquarters'. What this meant in essence was that I was enrolled back into the system but I had no portfolio. I thought perhaps a more specific assignment would come in time.

Nobody, no one at all, asked me about the eight years I had spent in captivity. Not even in a chatty, curious way. The Commander asked me no questions; my colleagues asked me no questions; I was not questioned by Naval Intelligence, Military Intelligence or National Intelligence. I felt I had seen the colour of the Tiger. They could have gathered so much information from me but they didn't ask. I was never summoned and I decided I did not need to go forward, voluntarily.

What they did do was to send me to a psychiatrist for assessment. After my third visit, the doctor said to me 'Commander, you don't come anymore. You send me the man who is sending you'. I realised that everyone in the Navy was sure I had sold out to the LTTE.

There was nothing for me to do. As a prisoner you can spend days doing nothing but out in society it's much harder to do that. In captivity, it's enough to be a man alive. Out in the world, it isn't. Not to do anything is frustrating. I had no hours, no desk, no place to be, no work to do. They gave me a staff car but no naval appointment.

I would arrive each morning and spend a little time sitting in the offices of friends. I would sit for a little with my friend Tissera—the man who had been a devoted surrogate father to my children in my absence—then Director of Naval Operations. But I knew I was disturbing him so then I would go and see another friend who was the Director of Naval Supplies. Soon I would take my leave of him too and read the paper in the Ward room. I'd have lunch and return home about two or three in the afternoon. Occasionally, I'd see Vijitha around. He had been inducted back into full service and happened to be serving at Headquarters at the time.

Were they trying to be humane, you ask? I don't think so. Then they should have told me? They should have said we're not going to ask too much of you, you have a rest and then come back. Treat it as disembarkation leave. They didn't say anything like that. They didn't ask me how I felt about it. I would have preferred to work. I had been doing nothing for eight years. I didn't need a rest.

I didn't even have a uniform to wear. I used to love wearing my naval uniform. Now I had come back to find my juniors promoted above me while my promotions had been withheld. I was not going to wear three stripes when I was due for more. So I didn't wear a uniform.

Rumours, of course, were rife. A friend in the Navy had saved me a few official intelligence reports. One indicated I had been seen riding a motorcycle around the Vanni, where I was training LTTE cadres with Soosai.

You remember I look exactly like my older brother. He worked as a field instructor for Ceylon Tobacco in the leaf division and travelled a lot between Dambulla and Kandy. Maybe this is where the rumour started that I made regular trips south from Vavuniya in Tobacco trucks. Once my brother stopped at a small wayside shop that happened to be run by a retired sailor. The shopkeeper said to him 'you'd better not be seen out in the open—you're a wanted man, you may be arrested'. My brother was taken aback but then realised what the man was thinking. He told him, 'I'm not Ajith, I'm Lalith'.

It was said the LTTE had opened a bank account for me in Nugegoda. A branch address and account number were printed in the papers. The account number was false. I think this particular story was not an accident but a wilful fabrication, though my younger brother did live in Nugegoda at the time. There were reports that the LTTE were making arrangements to send me and my family to Australia.

My father, a lifelong SLFP supporter, had once visited a Cabinet Minister of his party, to appeal for efforts to secure my release. A naval colleague of mine had got an appointment for my father and my wife to meet him. They had waited hours. The Minister finally came out and said to them something like 'Ah, Boyagoda—don't say anything about Boyagoda. Only yesterday I watched a tape with Madam and Boyagoda was leading the LTTE attack on Mullaitivu'. At the time of the Mullaitivu attack I was in a 3x10 foot prison cell in Periyamadu with two other men, squeezing out the sweat from our vests. My father told my wife that it was only for his son he restrained himself from hitting the man. I think about this now when someone says they've seen someone who disappeared. They've done it in Parliament; even the courts.

I suppose I was lucky not to hear some of these stories until I came home. They may have wanted to spare me. Also political comment in letters was censored, as a matter of routine, accord-

ing to ICRC protocols. I did sometimes receive letters with sec-
tions blacked out. I wrote to caution my family against asking
politicians favours on my behalf. These favours will come with
strings attached, I said.

But even while I was away I had known from my wife's letters
that my children were being bullied at school. It was mostly by
other children, often the sons of other servicemen and policemen. But sometimes even the teachers did it. At one point my
eldest son refused to go to school on account of the hostility he
faced there.

When I did come home I was angry and upset to hear the
things that had been said—and gradually just disgusted with
society. People give you more difficulties when you're already in
trouble. I don't know if it's something in our culture that makes
us feel a good story is less interesting than a bad one. Storytellers
concentrate on inventing gory detail to keep their audience
engaged. If you look at the rumours you can usually detect the
naivety inside of them. They assumed that since Soosai was
reported as capturing me, I must still be in his care. Didn't they
think the commander of the LTTE's entire sea operation might
have things to do besides look after a prisoner? Did they think
he would take my advice? Were the LTTE so stupid as to ask
their enemy to train them? Then again, some of the things they
described—like the siphoning and sale of naval diesel to the
Tigers—were also things that sometimes happened.

I never really got over this mistrust. Within a few months I
felt ready to be a fully functioning member of society but it
seemed that society would not accept me back. No one would
speak openly with me. No one really wanted to know what I had
seen, either. The only real question I was ever asked was how had
I been treated. Even strangers asked this. But gradually I began
to feel that they were not asking out of concern for me. They

were asking for a good story about the Tigers. They knew the answers they wanted.

I always said I had been treated humanely. This was the truth and it was also all I was prepared to say. I had been in this war; imprisoned by it. I had no intention of fuelling the fire of igno-rant animosity that kept the war alive. So, when the media asked me questions I told them my stories of Newton and of George Uncle, the translator. These were also true stories and stories that meant something to me. I think the conjecture was then made that I must have been helping the Tigers for them to treat me well. Or perhaps truth was just irrelevant.

My experiences with the Tigers were my experiences with the Tigers. Others have written of theirs and been called biased. But I always respect stories told with first-hand knowledge, whatever their bias. There were many others who wrote just by imagining. There were defence writers who wrote their articles entirely out of *Jane's Fighting Ships*. I remember stories of the Tigers using surface-to-air missiles that were written in the 1990s—though the fact was only really verified nearly twenty years later. But mostly, the people I met wanted to believe that the Tigers were monsters without exception—it reinforced their prejudices and kept the war going. I know the Tigers were capable of great brutality. There are many who can testify to this and many who did not survive it. My experience was not so bad. So, no one believed me.

For years, I resisted calls to political meetings. That was not the game I wanted to play. My family had always supported the SLFP but I did feel obliged to the UNP for securing my release. I finally agreed to attend a UNP rally. I said I would just come along. When I arrived, I discovered that there was a seat for me on stage. This was before the Presidential Election in 2010. By the position of my seat, I found myself endorsing the controversial candidature of Sarath Fonseka.[38] Once again I was called 'that Boyagoda'; a dubious bogeyman. The talk re-started about my having worked with the Tigers. Some of my old friends started to keep their distance.

Even some time later, I received an unexpected call. A man calling himself Murali said he had found me on Facebook and managed to locate a telephone number for me. He was calling from Canada. When he described who he was I realised that he was Oppilan, one of my teenage interrogators from my early captivity. But he said he had put all that behind him and wished to be known as Murali now. He told me a story I'd never expected. He said that at the time he was working in LTTE intelligence he was also simultaneously working for India's intelligence body, RAW. RAW had blackmailed him into service by threatening to expose a love affair that was forbidden under LTTE rules. Murali had subsequently worked for the intelligence services of the Sri Lankan forces in return for passage out of the country. I have a bad feeling he used stories about me as a calling card there. I wonder if this was another factor that contributed to the rumours about me. He sent me an account of his story that I cannot quite bring myself to read.

38

At the start I still thought things might change. I expected the Navy to reconvene the Board of Enquiry into the sinking of the *Sagarawardene*—this time to hear my own representation and decide whether I was guilty and due for a court martial. While I was in captivity, Selvaratnam had asked me what would happen next. He was curious and concerned about the sentence I might have to face when I got back. In fact the sentence was one of suspense. Nothing seemed to be happening at all.

After a while, I brought it up with the Commander of the Navy. While I was away, I had been found guilty of wilful negligence for anchoring my ship in one place and putting the vessel and its men in danger. On my return, I had contacted a friend of a friend who worked in the Attorney General's department. I'd learnt that it was against the principles of natural justice to find a man guilty without hearing his case. If I was found guilty after my case was heard, I would be due for court martial. A court martial in the Sri Lankan Navy proceeded like a case in the civil court—I could be represented by counsel and call witnesses. If I was found guilty, the maximum sentence would be life imprisonment.

It may sound ironic to you that a man released from captivity might risk it a second time. But the situation I was in I found more unbearable. It was important to me that I have official justice—whether or not I was found guilty. I wanted my children to know for sure if their father had been found to be a traitor. It isn't that my children doubted me. Once I was home, they considered the story over. But I wanted them to know, on more than my word.

When I brought it up with the Commander, he did not resist it. He said he would look into it and after some time a Board was indeed appointed. Once a Board was appointed the usual protocols drove it forward. The Board was made up of senior naval officers, as is customary. It issued me with a charge sheet, listing the allegations against me. I was accused of negligence and of exposing a naval vessel and its crew to danger. Witnesses would be asked to support or refute the allegations.

Within a few weeks, there was a hearing. I came to it very well prepared. My purpose was to establish that there was a reason I had kept my ship anchored in one place for so long on 19 September 1994. My witnesses were the ship's Communicator and two additional officers who had been on board. These men were very lucky to be alive and I was extremely fortunate that they were able to testify for me. We had not forgotten how many others we lost that night.

The Communicator confirmed that a stationary position report had been filed, according to the correct protocols. No one had asked us to move. Then, there was a claim that an intelligence report had been sent to the *Sagarawardene*, to warn us of imminent danger. The Communicator asserted repeatedly that no such report had been received. We had another stroke of luck here—the ship's logbook had survived the attack and no receipt was recorded there.

A Board of Enquiry like this takes place behind closed doors, with a stenographer present. Witnesses make their statements and then the Board takes the evidence away to analyse, before making a final report. I think the whole process took under two weeks. A report came back indicating I had been exonerated of all charges and no new charges had been brought against me. I was now a man officially free of allegation. My children were not the sons of a traitor.

Of course, this was only known to the Board itself, the Commander and anyone I told. But now, as far as I could see, there was no reason for me not to be inducted back into active service. Vijitha had been restored. All the Army guys were also reinstated; some of them are still serving today. Some of them even went back to the battlefront.

But for me, everything had stopped. It was like I had come back from the grave and the people around me were surprised and did not know what to do with me. True: I was an officer and so my case was a little different. But I had not surrendered to the LTTE; I was still a loyal serviceman. It was pure conjecture to suppose me a traitor. There was no way to certify my loyalty to my force except for the Navy to ask the Tigers and trust their word. They didn't ask for mine.

They could not ask me to leave the service, with no strike against my name. But, for a year and a half, my promotions were withheld and no job was given to me. Nor was I asking for a lot. I had thought carefully about how to make a request that would not cause problems for any other officer. I merely asked to be promoted to the level of the last promoted (or lowest ranking) of my batchmates. I was willing to be the lowest common denominator but not to be overlooked. I wanted the rank, medals and ribbons to which I was entitled.

Finally the Commander told me that my promotions would be given to me if I put in my papers for voluntary retirement. They were offering me now the retirement they'd refused when I applied for it nearly a decade earlier.

They dated my promotion and my retirement to coincide. I had to point out to them that this would nullify the benefits attending the promotion. My naval pay, for example, would not change. They then corrected it so that my retirement would follow my promotion by just a few days.

I felt that when I returned to the Navy, everything that came to me was something I had to ask for, to fight for. It was making me miserable. It's true that the Navy I returned to was not the one I had known. It was a huge professional force now. I felt that the Navy I had known and served in was a better one, but perhaps they did not. Perhaps they thought I would not fit into the new way of doing things. But they neither voiced their reservations nor gave me a chance to try.

I feel they should have told me what they were thinking. I feel the same way about their mistrust. If they had addressed it we could have discussed it. Maybe then they would have come to see things differently. In a sense, I returned from captivity to discover that I was more mistrusted by my own side than I had been by the enemy. At least you expect bad treatment from an enemy—so whenever I suffered in LTTE custody, I figured it was fair enough. When I suffered within my own force, I was hurt. I was a naval man—these things mattered to me.

For me, it was a new world, when I left the Navy. In the forces you always have people working for you. You command others to complete the tasks required. I was fifty before I learnt how civilians have personal workloads. I now learnt to work with others by entreaty rather than command. I learnt about politeness and tact. I learnt that people could say no. All the same, it was the self-discipline I learnt in the Navy that also helped me to change in the ways that were now necessary.

I enjoyed my new life. I was working for a company funding small and medium scale entrepreneurs who could not access bank loans. I travelled all over the country, meeting many different people and seeing the way they lived. I could spot a need for new projects and get them going. I came to recognise that hearing other people's grievances can feel harder than having your own. You see military training produces people who live alike and think alike. Now I was surrounded by people of vastly different experiences and opinions. When the tsunami[39] came our efforts were redoubled and my work took me further afield. I believe that I was being watched at times, suspected of sympathies with the LTTE.

I did not lose my connection to the Navy altogether. That was my community of friends and colleagues; these were the people who had cared for my family in my absence. We met frequently at batch get-togethers. I re-joined my extended family too. My wife's relatives are a clan who gathered together often and we would travel south for their reunions. We lived in a house with a beautiful garden. On my return, I told my wife it felt like a hotel. There was much to enjoy.

So, I did get back to a life of my own. It wasn't until I retired from the Navy that I started to feel more relaxed and able to get over my discomfort. When you ask me about it now, looking back, I don't think the transition took that long. But it felt longer while I was going through it.

It's harder to accept some things. I get hurt and irritable sometimes when my sons ask their mother to be an intermediary about things they need from me. I say to them, 'why can't you ask me, directly?' But it isn't really fair to expect it. The things that happen to us in childhood shape the rest of our lives. The traits that helped me to survive my captivity were drawn from my own steady childhood. I still regret that I was not around to pass these on to my boys, in turn.

They're grown up now. In 2011, my eldest, Shamal, got married, with his brother Manil as his best man. Later the same year, we were struck by tragedy. My middle son Manil was killed in a road accident. He was twenty-four at the time. At the funeral, some of my naval colleagues could not bear to look at his coffin. They had been stand-in fathers to my boys while I was away, trying to make sure they lost as little as possible. They could not believe that after all that, such a thing could have happened.

Manil had always been close to and kind to his mother. And in the years before he died, he had started chatting with me and asking for my opinion on things. He would tell me about things that happened at work, to hear my reflections on them. My eldest, Shamal, is now a father himself and so I think he also looks to his

own father more than he did before. His little daughter Anya—
our first grandchild—comes to us on weekdays. And they've just
had a new baby boy, Chanuk. Lahiru, my youngest, is doing a
degree in marketing and management. He also works with me in
my new business, breeding and exporting tropical fish.

40

But I wanted to say this to you also. We are made to change and change again, to adapt to the thing that we're in.

I spent my 40s in captivity—the years in which you are ready to do something in the world. I don't know what I might have made of these years I had I not been a prisoner then. Being a prisoner changed my character and simplified my aspirations when I came back. I regretted that I had been away from my family so much, even before I was captured. I felt my priorities had been wrong. I came back determined to be a better husband and a better father. For a while I did try to be that.

But then I got absorbed again. I changed back into being a man in the world. I got caught up at work and spent less time at home. I was working in a new world to the one I had known before, but in the end it belonged to the same culture. What is that thing they say? 'A good employee is a bad husband?' It's a terrible thing, really. Sometimes I wonder now how well I have managed to keep my resolutions.

You lose everything when you become a prisoner. At first you still have egoistic feelings. But each time they rise in an incident, you realise you must give more of them up. Gradually, you lose all ego. Then you come back into society and you find that the values you gave up are the ones you're meant to live by. There are many competing ideologies; there are many ways of behaving: you have to choose between them. You define yourself by your choices. Perhaps it's human nature that hubris rises in free men. I was never very ambitious either before or after, but I learnt to live again in that world.

As for my story, everyone got over it. Once they'd seen the half hour interviews and read the serialised fabrications, their curiosity was satisfied. Very occasionally, over a drink, someone I know well will ask me more. Then, in the moment, I find myself saying a little more than I have said before and suddenly my listener registers something new. He will say to me 'I'm so glad I asked you about that, now I understand so much more'.

Maybe that is partly why I wanted to write this book. When I first came back I made a choice to say less, so that my story would not be sensationalised. In fact people sensationalised it anyway, in the ways that they wanted. I watched this unfold, unsure what I could do to stop it. The thing is—my story began and ended in two completely different countries. I was caught between the two, not knowing my way.

EPILOGUE

We exchange worlds. On a day to day basis I don't really think back to that time unless there is an incident that reminds me. When I heard reports from the North and East, especially during the final years of the war, then I would remember my time there. I still think about all those people I knew in captivity. I know that George Uncle, the translator, surrendered at the end of the war. I believe he is now released from custody. I used to listen to the announcements of the dead on the war reports, to see if I knew anyone among the names read out. It did happen sometimes. I believe I heard when Selvaratnam was killed.

I have no idea what happened to Reuben or Mohan. I imagine some of the lower ranking cadres survived or went through the Government rehabilitation processes. The problem with these processes is thinking it is possible to draw lines between the people and the LTTE. You have to understand that it's impossible to do that. If you were from those areas you might not like the LTTE but the movement still came from the circles of your community; your neighbours, your friends, your family. Then you cannot renounce them. Even if you have faced terrible hardships and brutality at their hands, maybe you cannot renounce them.

At the end of the war, I was relieved the war itself was over. At least the part of the conflict that was an outright war had come to an end. I had to be relieved about that. I could stop fearing that someone I knew would be blown up on a bus in Colombo. That was some consolation—I don't want to forget that.

But I was aware of so many lives that had been lost or ruined—people I knew and thousands more I did not know. There is absolutely no victory in a war—I'm sure of that. I sometimes think about this war as a fight between brothers. It took decades to separate these communities completely and it will take decades to bring them together.

There are good signs of late that change is on its way; that we will progress beyond *avurudhu utsavayas*[40] in the Vanni and super-luxury apartments in Jaffna. Those were never the things that were missing. Truth is, too many people still think in racial terms and for that to change it will take some time and political risk. I hear people question the new Opposition in Parliament. They say now the Tamil nationalists have lost at war, they're trying to win by argument. They forget that we were here before and failed; that there might never have been a war if we'd done better in Parliament all those long years ago. But perhaps we are wiser now and know we have to create the context for change. We have to start sometime to turn the end of war into peace.

* * *

I did meet the others occasionally, afterwards. Gamini got married, Sisira got married. I went to their weddings. I helped Nomis a little and Anura's wife after he was killed. He had gone back to war and was killed when he was travelling in a bus that hit a landmine. For a while I had enough contact with my fellow prisoners to have some idea of what was happening in their lives. But we didn't meet often. Everyone was preoccupied with his own transition.

Vijitha keeps in touch of course. I only see him very occasionally now. We bump into each other at hospitals—that sort of thing.

We spoke recently across a barrier at the airport. He was on his way to Dubai to join a ship, working for a company providing security against pirates. When he first came home he returned to the Navy but eventually retired with a back ailment. He had two more daughters. His daughters are three studious girls. When my son died, Vijitha was present at all our ceremonies.

Amerasinghe also calls. Some of the others came to my son's funeral. Some I've not met in years. But our lives went in different ways. We had a shared experience—and an unusual one—but you have also to remember that there are other things that affect the quality of the sharing. I was so much older than my fellow prisoners that our experiences were not so easily communicated. Emerging into the world as young men they also had to start from scratch, especially as they came from poorer families than I did. We'd been together in captivity but we inhabited different parts of the world outside. Vijitha always said we were like travellers on a train. We'd spent the journey together but we all got off at different stops.

* * *

For a few years after my release I didn't go anywhere near where I had been held captive. Then, after the tsunami, I was asked to travel to the North with my company, taking relief supplies of clothes, food rations and clearing gear like tractors and trailers. We went to Vavuniya and then on to Kilinochchi—the reverse of the journey I'd made on the day of my release. I had a mixed set of feelings going back and this time as a civilian.

We were handing over our goods to the LTTE, since it was they who administered the area. Arrangements had been made to give us quick clearances. We talked to the ICRC and we talked to the LTTE. Remember, during the ceasefire there was an official Peace Secretariat in the Vanni. You could call from Colombo and ask to be put through to the LTTE political office.

I mean the strangest things happened during that time—
strange only because we were used to wartime conditions. Once
I was standing in a queue at the Dialog office on Union Place in
Colombo. I was there to pay my phone bill and I caught sight of
a familiar face. Pulidevan[41] said to me 'Ah, Captain, how?' This
man was a high ranking LTTE officer. I knew him from my days
of going to ICRC meetings at the LTTE political offices in
Jaffna. It was such a surprise to see him moving freely about
Colombo. 'What are you doing here?' I asked him. 'I came to pay
my telephone bill,' he said. He showed me his phone as he said
it. It was of course a phone with satellite communication, since
there were then no mobile towers in the Vanni.

When I travelled north with my company, we had to deliver
our relief supplies to the LTTE political headquarters. There
may have been a ceasefire but this was still an LTTE controlled
area and they were the official administration. The LTTE had,
characteristically, arranged for press and TV people to record the
reception of goods. (Of course news stories followed in the
South, about my taking goods back to the Tigers).

Everyone greeted me. Suda Master and Daya Master were
there, as I had expected, but I couldn't see George Uncle. When
I asked where he was, I was told that his wife had just died. I
asked if it would be alright to visit him. I was told of course it
would be fine. They gave us directions and in the evening I set
off to find the place.

We couldn't drive all the way up to the house. At some point
I had to get down and walk. There was no electricity but I could
just make out figures on the verandah, by the light of petromax
lamps. I recognised George from a distance. He was talking to
some people. The dogs barked at our approach and everyone
looked up. George walked forward trying to make out who it
was. As he recognised me, he opened out his arms. He said

'Ajith, is it really you I'm seeing?' He said I was the last person he expected that night.

George Uncle's eyes filled with tears and he called to his children who had come for the funeral from Australia and Canada and all those places. He said that even in his grief he was so pleased to see me. He told his children who I was and how, even after being his prisoner, I had come to see him. I laughed and said 'this is the way in Sinhala culture—we don't hold grudges'. I knew he had a lot of affection for the South from his years as a post-master in Sabaragamuwa. But really, I was also very moved to be there that day. We talked together for about an hour.

* * *

And then there was the time I saw Newton.

I'd gone up to Elephant Pass to hand over some fishing boats as part of another relief programme. On my return to the LTTE political office, they told me someone was waiting to meet me, and led me to a different place. Newton was there with another cadre who had been a constant companion, even before. And Newton was carrying a child—his new son, about a year and a half old at that time. We shook hands. He said he'd heard I was in the area and he wanted his youngest child to meet me too. He must have travelled over an hour by motorbike to come from Mullaitivu to Kilinochchi, just for this purpose.

I was so moved. I had never done anything for Newton; he was in no way obliged to me. It was a gesture of pure friendship. I was pleased to see him too of course. He was such a mild man at heart and we had always been friends. We talked and drank tea together. Other people took photographs for us. Newton must have been in his mid-30s by then, I in my early 50s.

I'm unlikely ever to see him again. I read in the papers that about a year before the war ended, Newton came to the South and then went missing. Maybe he managed to leave the country. Maybe he was captured. I am not very hopeful for him if he was. When we've seen journalists disappear, it is hard to have hope for a noted separatist. I think about Newton's daughter saying 'our Appa can't leave the Vanni; he will be arrested' and I wonder if Newton's wife is possibly managing alone now, as my wife did while I was in captivity. I hope the family are alive.

You asked me once what the hardest thing was about captivity. Most of it was pretty hard, really. The whole experience was a test. But despite the suffering, I don't feel sad when I think about those years. I got to see something not many people got to see. It's possible no one will ever experience that again. I hope no one will. But it also makes me feel like I was given a privileged insight. I can even feel happy about it. It was an experience that added something to my life even as it took other things away. If I didn't see it like this, how would I live with it?

NOTES

NOTES

CHAPTER 1

1. A *mahanayake* is a high priest of the Buddhist clergy.
2. Buddhism has long been the majority religion amongst the majority Sinhala community in Sri Lanka—with 'Sinhala Buddhist' becoming a byword for the establishment. The term is used both earnestly and ironically.

CHAPTER 2

3. A half-loaf of bread, a spicy coconut relish and beef curry.
4. String-hoppers/indi-appa (S)/iddiyappam (T) are rice noodle cakes.
5. A distilled liquor widely consumed in Sri Lanka, made from the fermented sap of the coconut flower.

CHAPTER 5

6. On 23 July 1983, the Liberation Tigers of Tamil Eelam, still a fledgling separatist force, ambushed and killed 13 soldiers of the Sri Lankan Army. In the South, tensions mounted around the return of the soldiers' bodies to their families. Riots broke out and organised mobs also began to operate. Sometimes armed with electoral lists that identified the ethnicity of household occupants, they set about looting and destroying the homes and businesses of Tamil people. Between 300–3000 people were killed over the course of a week and many more homes and businesses ruined. Up to 200,000 people were made homeless. The Government was unable or unwilling to contain the riot. Only on the 5th day did the President make a public address calling for an end to the violence. The Government's ineffective response

and the systematic organisation of the mobs are customarily taken as evidence that Black July—as it is sometimes now known—was a government condoned pogrom against the Tamil people of Sri Lanka. Following the riots, many Tamil people fled the country, others fled the South. The LTTE (along with other militant groups) grew exponentially, both in support and cadre. This event is commonly taken to mark the beginning of full-scale hostilities between the Sri Lankan state and the separatist movements.

7. Kovil means temple in the Tamil language; the word is used for temples and churches of all religions. In Sinhala and in some Sri Lankan English usages it is, as here, taken to mean specifically a Hindu temple.

8. Wellawatte and Bambalapitiya are two adjoining neighbourhoods of central Colombo. Wellawatte is known as a neighbourhood with predominantly Tamil residents.

9. The fight for a separate state sought to establish a Tamil homeland in the north and east of the island, already the area with the greatest concentration of Tamil peoples.

CHAPTER 6

10. A vada/vade is a fritter made from lentils or other pulses, eaten South India and Sri Lanka. The flattened 'Point Pedro vada' is an eccentric variation on the usual shape.

11. Thosai is a Sinhala pronounciation of dosai or dosa, the pancake made of fermented rice and gram flour that is a part of South Indian and Sri Lankan Tamil cuisine. Idli is a softer steamed staple, made from similar ingredients.

CHAPTER 7

12. Deputy Inspector General
13. A *pada yatra* is a pilgrimage by foot; a term used for both religious and protest pilgrimages.

CHAPTER 9

14. The International Committee of the Red Cross is a worldwide humanitarian organisation intended to act as a neutral body in situations of armed conflict. The ICRC is the international body most often associated with representing the interests of prisoners of war.

15. Panadol is the brand of paracetamol most commonly used in Sri Lanka.

16. 'Amma' means mother in both Tamil and Sinhala and is also a way of respectfully addressing an older woman, in both languages.

CHAPTER 12

17. Thillaiyampalam Sivanesan, or Colonel Soosai, commanded the naval wing of the LTTE, also known as the Sea Tigers.

CHAPTER 13

18. The term Black Tiger distinguishes the LTTE's cadres trained for suicide missions. Black Sea Tigers were then Black Tigers of the LTTE's naval wing.

CHAPTER 14

19. A bright pink, sweet fizzy drink famously beloved by children in Sri Lanka.

20. Ranasinghe Premadasa was President of Sri Lanka from 1989 until May 1993 (when he was assassinated by the LTTE). He is said to have supplied arms to the Tigers in a bid to force out the Indian Peace Keeping Force.

21. Shopkeeper/merchant.

CHAPTER 15

22. Iddiyappam (string-hoppers) and pittu, like idli and thosai, are staple foods made with rice flour and eaten with curries, in Sri Lanka.

23. Tamil Eelam was the name given to the separate state for which the LTTE, the Liberation Tigers of Tamil Eelam, were fighting in the north and east of the island.

CHAPTER 16

24. Vinayagamoorthy Muralitharan or Colonel Karuna Amman was at this time a high ranking member of the LTTE, the Leader's bodyguard and deputy and the LTTE's Eastern Commander. In 2004, he famously left the LTTE. His Karuna Faction later joined with Government forces to defeat the LTTE in the East. Popularly known and mistrusted as 'Karuna', he later became a Member of Parliament.

CHAPTER 17

25. 'Appa' means father.

CHAPTER 19

26. An interjection of pity frequently used in Sinhala conversation.

CHAPTER 20

27. The Nallur Kandasamy Kovil is an important Hindu temple in Jaffna and also a landmark by which outsiders orient themselves.

CHAPTER 23

28. The Vanni is the name given to a northern area of the Sri Lankan mainland. In everyday conversations about the war, it is a term often used loosely to mean the jungle, the war zone and the unknown.

CHAPTER 26

29. A mammoty is a kind of garden hoe—with a broad blade—used in Sri Lanka and India.
30. A specific version of *pirith* (as it is known in Sinhala): incantations of the word of the Buddha, recited as a form of shelter and protection.

CHAPTER 27

31. The term of greeting in Tamil that is known by many Sinhala speakers.

CHAPTER 28

32. The Sri Lankan New Year is an annual harvest festival—and an all important holiday in both the Sinhala and Tamil communities.
33. Milk rice—a dish of rice cooked in coconut milk—served on auspicious occasions.
34. Vesak is the most important full moon of the year for Sri Lankan—and other—Buddhists, marking the Buddha's birth and enlightenment.

CHAPTER 30

35. S.P. Thamilselvan (or Thamilchelvan) was at the time a prominent political leader in the movement and a national and international negotiator for the LTTE. He rose in prominence in these roles in later years, before he was killed near Kilinochchi in 2007, in a precision airstrike by Government forces.

CHAPTER 35

36. Tiger cadres were popularly known to wear cyanide capsules around their necks which they would swallow in the event of falling into enemy hands.

37. A pottu (or bindi) is a small ornament, signifying the 'third eye,' worn by women on their foreheads. Traditionally, Tamil women will wear a red pottu after they are married and not remove it unless their husbands die. The pottu has commonly been used, especially during the war, as an identifier of ethnicity.

CHAPTER 37

38. Sarath Fonseka was the Commander of the Sri Lankan Army when it defeated the Tamil Tigers in May 2009. The following year he ran for Presidential Election against the incumbent President, Mahinda Rajapaksa, who had been his Commander-in-Chief.

CHAPTER 39

39. Many coastal areas of Sri Lanka were devastated by the 2004 Indian Ocean tsunami. At official count: 30,957 people killed and 5,637 missing.

EPILOGUE

40. Annual festivities to mark the Sri Lankan New Year, organised by local communities and also by the State, in different parts of the country.

41. Seevaratnam Pulidevan was the head of the LTTE's Peace Secretariat during the ceasefire. He was also killed in the final battles of the war.

ACKNOWLEDGMENTS

(Ajith Boyagoda)

I thank my parents, my mother-in-law and other extended family members for their encouragement.

I owe a deep gratitude to my wife Chani for being with me in all odd weathers so I could tell this story—and to my sons, Shamal, Manil and Lahiru for their tolerance.

I gratefully acknowledge Anthony Motha who once began working with me on another telling of this story. Although he and I had to put that account aside, I am grateful to him for the impetus he gave me to re-tell my story.

Cdr Somasiri Devendra encouraged me to tell this story and found those who could help me to do it. He introduced me to Sam Perera and Ameena Hussein who in turn introduced me to Sunila Galappatti.

A big thank you to Sunila for her commitment, dedication and patience—without which you would not be reading this book.

Finally I thank all those who have encouraged and inspired me to recount this experience.

ACKNOWLEDGEMENTS

(Sunila Galappatti)

My first thanks must go to Ameena Hussein and Sam Perera for introducing me to Commodore Boyagoda. I owe them a debt for suggesting our collaboration, especially when we did not take the book back to their publishing house. Cdr Somasiri Devendra played an important role in that initial introduction and has remained interested in the project throughout.

Above all, I thank Commodore Ajith Boyagoda for trusting me to write his story; patiently telling and re-telling it as I asked. I thank him too for the generous spirit in which he re-read my telling of his story. Along with him, Mrs Boyagoda, who made time to sit with me and tell a part of hers.

* * *

I am grateful to friends who remained alongside while I worked on this book, over the course of nearly five years. In particular, Menika van der Poorten, Lalin Dias and Ruwani Wijayanandana, Michael Meyler, Subha Wijesiriwardena, Sam Soundy and, later in the process, Kate and Daniel Murray, Veena Joory, Roger Mortlock, Blandine Chambost.

Warm thanks also to Sanjaya Senanayake, Marilyn Weaver, Morgan Meis and Stefany Anne Golberg, Chulani Kodikara and

Vijay Nagaraj, Steve Russell, Sonali Deraniyagala, Kiran Kothari, Michael Collyer and Dulani Kulasinghe, Alan Keenan, Smriti Daniel, Rana Dasgupta, Ed Wollaston, Jeanie O'Hare, Lucy Hannah, Jeremy Herrin, David Norgrove.

Among these friends and family there are those I must acknowledge in detail for the part they played at different moments in the writing of this book: Sunila Abeysekera for persuading me I was equal to this task; Mirak Raheem for thoughtful—and lasting—reflections on the exercise; Shanthi Thambaiah and Neelakandan Dharmaretnam for their interest, ongoing conversation and extraordinary hospitality. I thank T. Shanaathanan for generous conversation and a rare sensibility of heart and mind; Sarala Emmanuel, for sisterly advice; and Ananda Galappatti, whose opinion is especially important to me.

I am enormously grateful to Michael Ondaatje for being the best champion that this book or I could want. His ear for the nuance of the book and his belief in it played a special role in propelling it to completion. Michael led me to Ellen Levine and Claire Roberts, who also did their best for it.

Then Michael Dwyer and everyone at Hurst, for taking the book on its own terms; accepting that it was a book written first for those who knew this war and then for those who did not.

My very deepest gratitude goes to Ranjit and Janaki Galappatti. To them, more than anyone else, I have gone for advice and discussion—always humane, always interested and always ready to go on a road-trip. Theirs is life-giving belief, support and friendship.

(Podi) Kusal Perera I met as I finished writing. He joined me there and he never wavers.